Contents

Introduction

By becoming a Brownie Girl Scout leader you have embarked on a wonderful journey that promises to take you to new places (platform tents, perhaps!), teach you new ideas (the adjective "bad" really means "good," maybe?), and enable you to make an indelible impression on the lives of youngsters. Your support may encourage a shy child to someday become a group leader.

Many times children seek role models outside their families. This can be you. With a sense of humor and lots of patience, you can open doors for girls at an early age and help them to acquire skills and interests that they will take with them into the future.

Along with the innumerable rewards of being a Girl Scout leader come the challenges. Interacting with a

THE GUIDE FOR BROWNIE GIRL SCOUT LEADERS

Girl Scouts of the USA
420 Fifth Avenue
New York, N.Y. 10018-2798

Girl Scouts®

National President
Connie L. Matsui

National Executive Director
Marsha Johnson Evans

National Director, Membership and Program
Sharon Woods Hussey

Director, Program Development
Harriet S. Mosatche, Ph.D.

Project Director
Harriet S. Mosatche, Ph.D.

Author
Rosemarie Cryan

Contributors
Chris Bergerson, Toni Eubanks, Libby Marks McDonell,
Lauraine Merlini, Harriet S. Mosatche, Ph.D., Patricia Paddock

Director of Publishing
Suzanna Penn

Senior Editor
David Sahatdjian

Designer
Kaeser and Wilson Design Ltd.

Illustrators
Eveline Feldmann Allred, p. 13; Richard A. Goldberg, pp. 32, 34, 40;
DJ Simison, pp. 8, 36, 38; Leigh Thompson, pp. 18, 29, 43, 45, 51;
Liz Wheaton, pp. 42, 44

Crafts
Kelly Bender

Photographers
Richard Blinkoff, pp. 3, 4 (top); Peter Brandt, cover, p. 41;
Lori Adamsky Peek, pp. 5, 6, 19, 25, 26, 27, 28 (left), 30, 31, 37, 55;
Andrea Sperling, p. 4 (bottom)

Inquiries related to *The Guide for Brownie Girl Scout Leaders* should be directed to Membership and Program, Girl Scouts of the USA, 420 Fifth Avenue, New York, N.Y. 10018-2798.

Permission is granted by Girl Scouts of the USA to photocopy the telephone contact list on page 18 and the meeting plan worksheet on page 24.

The article "How to Succeed in (Leader) Business" on pages 25–28 is reprinted by permission of *Girl Scout Leader*, fall 1998, © Girl Scouts of the USA.

group of six- to eight-year-olds might sometimes seem like you have stepped into the eye
of a hurricane. You may need to set parameters
to channel the boundless energy and high-
spirited exuberance that children frequently
exhibit when they are having fun, which is
what Girl Scouting is all about!

You are busy with multiple responsibilities
and commitments, but most of your time as a
Girl Scout leader should be spent enjoying activities and interacting with the girls, not doing lots of paperwork or attending
too many "adults only" meetings.

The first part of this book details essential Girl Scout information. Section II provides several charts and ideas that will help you to plan activities with girls. The third section contains a series of fictitious scenarios and suggestions for handling them as a Girl Scout leader. Section IV includes activities that you can do "in a pinch." The fifth, and final, section is an annotated resource list that will help you to choose the Girl Scout publications most appropriate for the activities that you are doing or the events that you are planning. A general list of other resources is also included in this part of the book.

Your trip has just begun. Settle in and you will discover that the girls in your troop have as many things to teach as they have to learn.

Basic Girl Scout Information

Girl Scout Program Goals

Four program goals serve as the bedrock for all the materials, activities, and initiatives that are developed under the auspices of Girl Scouting. They are as follows:

1

Girls will develop to their full potential. Girl Scouting will:

- Foster girls' feelings of self-acceptance and unique self-worth.
- Promote girls' perception of themselves as competent, responsible, and open to new experiences and challenges.
- Offer girls opportunities to learn new skills.
- Encourage girls' personal growth.
- Allow girls to utilize and practice talents and abilities.

2

Girls will relate to others with increasing understanding, skill, and respect. Girl Scouting will:

- Help girls develop sensitivity to others and respect for their needs, feelings, and rights.
- Promote an understanding and appreciation of individual, cultural, religious, and racial differences.
- Foster the ability to build friendships and working relationships.

3

Girls will develop a meaningful set of values to guide their actions and to provide the foundation for sound decision-making. Girl Scouting will:

- Help girls develop meaningful values and ethics that will guide their actions.
- Foster an ability to make decisions that are consistent with girls' values and that reflect respect for the rights and needs of others.
- Empower girls to act upon their values and convictions.
- Encourage girls to reexamine their ideals as they mature.

4

Girls will contribute to the improvement of society through the use of their abilities and leadership skills, working in cooperation with others. Girl Scouting will:

- Help girls develop concern for the well being of their communities.
- Promote girls' understanding of how the quality of community life affects every member of society.
- Encourage girls to use their skills to work with others for the benefit of all.

As a Brownie Girl Scout leader, you will find it helpful to keep the four Girl Scout program goals in mind when planning activities with the girls. Remembering the goals of Girl Scout program will help you build a balanced experience for girls.

Girl Scout Promise and Law

As a values-based organization, Girl Scouts finds its foundation in the Promise and Law. You can always rely on the principles found in them to help girls make decisions or relate to one another.

THE GIRL SCOUT PROMISE

On my honor, I will try:

To serve God and my country,
To help people at all times,
And to live by the Girl Scout Law.

THE GIRL SCOUT LAW

I will do my best to be

honest and fair,
friendly and helpful,
considerate and caring,
courageous and strong, and
responsible for what I say and do,

and to

respect myself and others,
respect authority,
use resources wisely,
make the world a better place, and
be a sister to every Girl Scout.

Age Levels in Girl Scouting

Brownie Girl Scouts are one of the five age levels in Girl Scouting. The other four are Daisy Girl Scouts, Junior Girl Scouts, Cadette Girl Scouts, and Senior Girl Scouts. Often you may hear someone say, "I was a Brownie, but I was never a Girl Scout!" Brownie Girl Scouts are six, seven, or eight years old or in first, second, or third grade. They are part of a worldwide movement that has members in more than 100 nations, all belonging to the World Association of Girl Guides and Girl Scouts (WAGGGS). The age levels are:

World Association (WAGGGS) pin

Daisy Girl Scouts

(grades K–1 or 5–6 years old)

Brownie Girl Scouts

(grades 1–3 or 6–8 years old)

Junior Girl Scouts

(grades 3–6 or 8–11 years old)

Cadette Girl Scouts

(grades 6–9 or 11–14 years old)

Senior Girl Scouts

(grades 9–12 or 14–17 years old)

Resources for Brownie Girl Scouts

Brownie Girl Scouts use two basic books—the *Brownie Girl Scout Handbook* and *Try-Its for Brownie Girl Scouts*. The handbook contains basic information about Girl Scouting and other topics important for six- to eight-year-olds to know—friends, families, community, safety, world citizenship, leadership, and the environment.

Try-Its for Brownie Girl Scouts is a companion book that offers activities to reinforce and extend the topics covered in the handbook. Girls earn Try-Its by doing activities and completing projects. They wear these awards on their uniforms.

For a fuller discussion of Girl Scout resources, see Section V, "Annotated List of Girl Scout Resources for Brownie Girl Scouts," pages 55-57.

TiPS for Using Brownie
Girl Scout Resources

The resources for Brownie Girl Scouts contain invaluable ideas for activities that are sure to captivate and stimulate youngsters. As such, you should use these books as a springboard for introducing girls to a wide range of topics and ideas while engaging them in as much activity as possible. The following tips will assist you in achieving this goal:

• Don't expect girls to read their handbooks cover to cover. Instead, they may read a few pages at one time and then skip to an entirely new topic by the next meeting. Similarly, girls may not want to complete an entire Try-It; they may do one activity and then decide that they want to move on to a different Try-It.

• Instructions written in simple language will work best because some Brownie Girl Scouts may not be entirely proficient at reading.

• If an activity in either the handbook or the Try-Its book seems way too advanced (or too easy) for the girls in your group, modify it to make it fun and educational for all involved.

• The girls in your troop are certain to have different interests and abilities. Vary activities enough so that the program meets the needs of all girls. Try sports one time and crafts the next, for example.

• Girl Scout meetings and activities should be distinctly different from school. Involve girls in the decision-making process as much as possible. Allow them freedom to make choices and to express their opinions.

• Establish guidelines and parameters for acceptable behavior from the very start of the troop year. See *Safety-Wise* for more information. Make sure you are using the most recent edition—at least the eighth printing.

Brownie Girl Scout Try-Its

The 57 Try-Its in *Try-Its for Brownie Girl Scouts* are designed to expose girls to new hobbies, skills, and fun activities. The emphasis is on trying new experiences, not gaining proficiency. When girls complete any four activities in a Try-It, they may receive the award to wear on their sashes or vests.

Ideally, the activities in the Try-Its will be done in a group. They are, however, flexible enough for girls to work on them alone or with just one other person. Many activities require adult assistance. Before introducing any Try-It to the girls in your troop or group, review it so that you know just what materials you will need, how long the activity will take, and what results you can expect.

Girls should not feel pressured to complete a Try-It if they are really not enjoying the activities. Encourage girls to sample Try-Its on topics that are unfamiliar to them.

It is perfectly acceptable to amend or adapt activities when special circumstances make it difficult to complete them as written. For example, girls may be asked to view an exhibit in a museum. If the closest museum is in the next town, county, or even state, this may not be possible. It would, therefore, be perfectly acceptable

for girls to visit a museum online or view artifacts at a local historical society or even an antiques store. Flexibility is essential when dealing with youngsters and completing Try-Its is no exception.

As the leader, you determine when a Try-It has been earned. Girls should not feel that they are in a race or competition to earn the most Try-Its. Each girl should receive equal praise for her efforts, whether she has earned one award or 10.

A Court of Awards, a ceremony to recognize girls' achievements, can be held to distribute Try-Its. You should plan this event with the girls in your troop.

Finally, earning Try-Its is only one aspect of the Girl Scout program for Brownie Girl Scouts and should not become the primary focus of all meetings. Girls should be encouraged to enjoy different types of activities, not just the ones that end with a tangible award.

Uniforms and Insignia

Use the following illustrations of the Brownie Girl Scout uniform and adult uniform as a guide for the placement of Girl Scout insignia.

❶ Brownie Girl Scout Pin

❷ World Association Pin

❸ Insignia tab

❹ Brownie council identification set

❺ Troop numerals

❻ Membership stars

❼ Discs for membership stars

❽ Bridge to Brownie Girl Scouts

❾ Try-Its

❶ Adult insignia tab

❷ World Trefoil Pin

❸ Adult Position Pin

❹ Girl Scout Pin

❺ Membership numeral guards

❻ Campus Girl Scout guard

❼ Appreciation Pin

❽ Thanks Badge

❾ Thanks Badge II

❿ Honor Pin

⓫ Lifetime Membership Pin

⓬ Personalized ID Pin

⓭ Girl Scout Gold Award

⓮ Bridge to Adult Girl Scouts

⓯ Years of Service Pin

⓰ Outstanding Volunteer Award Pin

⓱ Outstanding Leader Award Pin

Religious Awards

In addition to Try-Its, Brownie Girl Scouts may earn religious awards. Use the following information to contact the organizations that can help girls earn specific awards.

RELIGIOUS ORGANIZATION	AWARD	WHERE TO GET INFORMATION
BAHA'I	Unity of Mankind	Baha'I Committee on Scouting Baha'I National Center Wilmette, Ill. 60091 (708) 869-9039
BAPTIST	See awards listed under Protestant and Independent Christian Churches	P.R.A.Y. P.O. Box 6900, St. Louis, Mo. 63123 (800) 933-PRAY (7729)
BUDDHIST	Ages 6-8 Padma Award	Buddist Church of America National Headquarters 1710 Octavia Street, San Francisco, Calif. 94109 (415) 776-5600
CHRISTIAN SCIENCE		P.R.A.Y. P.O. Box 6900, St. Louis, Mo. 63123 (800) 933-PRAY (7729)
CHURCHES OF CHRIST	Joyful Servant Award	Members of Churches of Christ for Scouting ACU Station, Box 27618, Abilene, Texas 79699-7618 (915) 674-3739
EASTERN ORTHODOX		P.R.A.Y. P.O. Box 6900, St. Louis, Mo. 63123 (800) 933-PRAY (7729)
EPISCOPAL	Ages 6-8 Grades 1-3 God and Me	P.R.A.Y. P.O. Box 6900, St. Louis, Mo. 63123 (800) 933-PRAY (7729)
HINDU	Ages 6-8 Grades 1-3 Dharma Award	North American Hindu Association 46133 Amesbury Drive, Plymouth, Mich. 48170 (313) 453-5049 or 981-2323
ISLAMIC	Ages 5-8 Bismillah Award	Islamic Committee on Girl Scouting 31 Marian Street, Stamford, Conn. 06907 (203) 359-3593
JEWISH	Ages 6-9 Lehavah Award	National Jewish Girl Scout Committee of the Synagogue Council of America 327 Lexington Avenue, New York, N.Y. 10016 (212) 686-8670

RELIGIOUS ORGANIZATION	AWARD	WHERE TO GET INFORMATION
LUTHERAN	Ages 6-8 Grades 1-3 God and Me	P.R.A.Y. P.O. Box 6900, St. Louis, Mo. 63123 (800) 933-PRAY (7729)
(MORMON) CHURCH OF JESUS CHRIST OF LATTER-DAY SAINTS		Salt Lake District Center Church of Jesus Christ of Latter-Day Saints 1999 W. 1700 South, Salt Lake City, Utah 84104 (801) 240-2141
PROTESTANT AND INDEPENDENT CHRISTIAN CHURCHES	Ages 6-8 Grades 1-3 God and Me	P.R.A.Y. P.O. Box 6900, St. Louis, Mo. 63123 (800) 933-PRAY (7729)
(QUAKERS) SOCIETY OF FRIENDS	Ages 6-8 Grades 2-3 That of God	Friends Committee on Scouting c/o Dennis Clarke 85 Willowbrook Road, Cromwell, Conn. 06416 (203) 635-1706
REORGANIZED CHURCH OF JESUS CHRIST OF LATTER-DAY SAINTS	Age 8 Light of the World	Youth Ministries Office The Auditorium P.O. Box 1059, Independence, Mo. 64051 (816) 833-1000
ROMAN CATHOLIC CHURCH	Ages 7-9 Family of God	National Federation for Catholic Youth Ministry 3700-A Oakview Terrace, NE, Washington, D.C. 20017 Attn: Orders Clerk (202) 636-3825
UNITARIAN UNIVERSALIST		Unitarian Universalist 25 Beacon Street, Boston, Mass. 02108 (617) 742-2100
UNITY CHURCH	Ages 6-8 God in Me	Association of Unity Churches P.O. Box 610, Lee's Summit, Mo. 64063 (816) 524-7414

Safety-Wise

One of your major responsibilities as a Girl Scout leader is to provide for the safety and security of girls. As a result, all Girl Scout program activities must meet the standards and guidelines as stated in *Safety-Wise*, a book given to every Girl Scout troop or group. Refer to *Safety-Wise* frequently to answer your questions concerning procedures for activities in which the girls in your troop or group are involved.

Managing Money and Troop Money-Earning Activities

The program standards and guidelines in *Safety-Wise* state that troops or groups should be financed by dues, money-earning activities, and through a percentage of council-sponsored product sales.

Some troops or groups arrange activities for which they charge fees or sell products or services. Sample activities appropriate for this purpose can be found in *Safety-Wise*. Before girls participate in any money-earning activity, permission from a parent or guardian must be obtained. The money that is earned from these activities is placed in the troop treasury.

You must always obtain written permission from your Girl Scout council before starting any money-earning activity. People at your council can help you investigate the laws, regulations, or insurance requirements that may apply to activities that involve money.

TROOP BUDGETING

It is important for girls to be involved in the troop's budgeting and overall financial process so that they can understand how funds are being used. Although you will have to provide guidance and might have to make some final decisions, girls can discuss things like saving their money for a more expensive trip, pooling their money with others to do a service project, or spending their money on supplies. Girls enjoy opportunities to go to the bank to deposit group funds, to go on shopping trips, or to compare costs through newspaper advertisements or fliers before purchasing items. Although you handle the group funds, it is important to remember that it is the group's money.

The Girl Scout Cookie Sale

The cookie sale is part of the Girl Scout program and should be designed to enhance girls' decision-making, planning, and goal-setting skills. Information on cookie sales can be found in the *Brownie Girl Scout Handbook* and in *Safety-Wise*. Note that neither girls nor adults may sell Girl Scout Cookies on the Internet. However, girls can e-mail friends and family to let them know about the sale.

...ces

...portant phone numbers and addresses so that you

...SITE

LOC...

POISON CONTROL PHONE NUMBER

She Told a Friend and She Told a Friend and So On

Sometimes plans change and you need to get in touch with the parents or guardians of the girls in your troop in a hurry. Create a phone chain to help you expedite this process. You call the first person on the list and then each adult is responsible for making one or two calls. This will help you save the time and energy that it will take to contact every member of the troop.

name _____

telephone _____

e-mail _____

name _____

telephone _____

e-mail _____

name _____

telephone _____

e-mail _____

name _____

telephone _____

e-mail _____

name _____

telephone _____

e-mail _____

name _____

telephone _____

e-mail _____

name _____

telephone _____

e-mail _____

name _____

telephone _____

e-mail _____

name _____

telephone _____

e-mail _____

name _____

telephone _____

e-mail _____

name _____

telephone _____

e-mail _____

name _____

telephone _____

e-mail _____

Planning Activities, Events, and Outings

Developmental Characteristics of Brownie Girl Scouts

A general understanding of the developmental characteristics of Brownie Girl Scouts will facilitate your role as a leader. It will enable you to appreciate why girls behave as they do and how you can assist in their learning and growth processes. Remember that these are broad, general characteristics. Each girl is different and will proceed through developmental stages at her own pace.

COGNITIVE SKILLS
(thinking and language)

- Children are developing vocabulary at a high rate: written, spoken, and heard.
- Children start to read.
- Children are interested in make-believe and fantasy stories.
- Children often have vivid imaginations.

GROSS MOTOR SKILLS
(large muscle activities)

- Children can throw a ball.
- Children can skip.
- Children can roller-skate.
- Children can jump rope.

FINE MOTOR SKILLS
(finely tuned movements)

- Children can trace around hand.
- Children can draw rectangles, circles, squares, and triangles.
- Children can mold clay objects.
- Children can reproduce letters and words.

SOCIAL SKILLS

- Children enjoy playing in groups.
- Children start to demonstrate independence from their families.
- Children want to have lots of friends, but may also select one "best friend."
- Children begin social telephoning to friends.
- Children like to help others.

EMOTIONAL SKILLS

- Children's moods may change from minute to minute.
- Children need lots of praise and encouragement.
- Children react negatively to too much direction.
- Children are interested in the difference between good and bad.

List Sample Activities from Each of the Following Girl Scout Resources that Match Developmental Characteristics of Brownie Girl Scouts

	TRY-ITS FOR BROWNIE GIRL SCOUTS	FOLLOW THE READER
COGNITIVE SKILLS		
GROSS MOTOR SKILLS		
FINE MOTOR SKILLS		
SOCIAL SKILLS		
EMOTIONAL SKILLS		

Planning Troop Meetings

Brownie Girl Scout meetings should be scheduled to best meet your needs and the needs of the girls. Some troops or groups of Brownie Girl Scouts meet once every two months for three hours, others meet twice a month for 45 minutes, while others may meet once a week for one hour. Sometimes, one activity will take up the entire meeting. Other times you will do a few different things.

SAMPLE FORMAT FOR A MEETING

Although there is no one template for a Brownie Girl Scout meeting, many troops find the following format quite successful:

✓	Start-up
✓	Opening
✓	Business
✓	Activities
✓	Cleanup
✓	Closing

Use these ideas as a catalyst for your own creativity:

- Set out a number of song tapes and a tape recorder, so that girls may sing along or dance to the music.
- Have paper, crayons, or markers, and small strips of cardboard available. Girls can make bookmarks with these materials.
- Provide materials for a simple game.

For each part of the meeting, you will need to consider which girls will be in charge and what supplies or resources you might need.

Start-Up

Start-up activities are usually self-directed. Girls can do them alone or in pairs with minimal supervision. This gives leaders a chance to greet the girls and parents as they arrive.

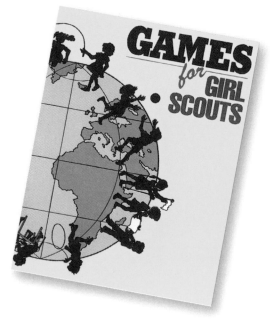

- Prepare a set of index cards so girls can practice "acting." The cards can have the names or pictures of animals, types of jobs, different emotions, historical characters (fictional and nonfictional), names of objects, or other sorts of categories. A girl picks a card and mimes the word she has chosen. The other girl, or the entire group, tries to guess the word on the card from the actions.
- Display a collection of children's magazines or books.
- Provide a box with simple games.

Opening

Opening activities should help the girls focus on the meeting and begin interacting as a group. A simple flag ceremony, a Girl Scout song such as "The Brownie Smile Song" or "Make New Friends," or a time set aside for sharing are some suggestions for suitable activities.

Business

Troop business might include making announcements, taking attendance, collecting dues or fees, planning for trips or activities, or making a new kaper chart. A kaper is a special Girl Scout word meaning "chore." A kaper chart is a simple way to rotate responsibilities. Girls can get to try out a variety of skills.

Activities

Besides the *Brownie Girl Scout Handbook* and *Try-Its for Brownie Girl Scouts*, there are other resources full of activities for the girls in your troop or group. See pages 55–57 for an annotated list.

When choosing an activity, it is important to look at it from a girl's perspective. There are other considerations, too. For example, is the activity suitable for your meeting place? Will the activity need to be adapted? Are there enough materials for each girl? Will you be able to clean up any messes?

Cleanup

The girls assigned to cleanup should have their names listed on a kaper chart. This assignment should be rotated among all the girls in the troop. It should never be used as a disciplinary tool, as girls need to know that cleaning up is a responsibility shared by all. It is not a punishment.

Closing

In the closing, emphasize what the girls have accomplished that day and what activities they can look forward to in the future. Good closing activities include:

- Gathering in a friendship circle and doing the friendship squeeze. (See page 19 of the *Brownie Girl Scout Handbook* for details.)

- Reciting the Girl Scout Promise and Law. Girls can take turns discussing the meaning of part of the Promise or Law, or describing something they have done that exemplifies them.

- Stating one personal goal that each girl would like to accomplish before the next meeting.

After the closing, be sure that you know how each girl will get home and that each girl is met by a parent or guardian.

Clean-Up Checker

Snacks

Supplies

Ceremonies

Closing Activity

It is often easier to plan a meeting if you have a set goal or a special theme. For example, if girls have expressed an interest in learning more about safety, your objective for the meeting may be to practice the fire safety procedures included in the *Brownie Girl Scout Handbook* on pages 62–63. You could extend this theme to a subsequent meeting by arranging a field trip to a firehouse, arranging for a guest speaker from a child abuse protection agency, or creating a first-aid kit with the girls.

Working from a written plan is often easier and more effective than improvising. The following worksheet is available for you to use in planning your meeting.

Meeting Plan Worksheet

	WHAT WE WILL DO	WHO WILL DO IT	WHAT WE NEED	NOTES
START-UP				
OPENING				
BUSINESS				
ACTIVITIES				
CLEANUP				
CLOSING				

Let's Get Organized

As you begin to work with your particular group of youngsters and their parents, you will, undoubtedly, establish your own system of organization. Read what one leader has to say:

"How to Succeed in (Leader) Business"

"What have I done?" and "Why have I done it?" were my first thoughts after agreeing to be the leader for my first grade daughter's Brownie Girl Scout troop. Two years and many meetings, camping adventures, and field trips later, my answers are the same, although I've often taken a side excursion to get there.

The "what" was the easier question to answer. I'd agreed to lead a troop of 12 lively first-grade girls into the world of Girl Scouting. It seemed a simple enough task.

But why had I committed to this task? Never mind that at 42 years old I was by far the oldest of the moms involved. Never mind that my only contact with Girl Scouting since 1968 (when my Cadette troop dissolved due to a lack of leadership and

interest) had been my annual Thin Mint purchase. I was doing this because my youngest daughter wanted to be a Girl Scout and I had no good reason to tell her no.

At first, the terminology threw me for a loop. What was a Try-It and when did Brownies start earning them? When did vests become an alternative to sashes, and where did all those

patches on the back come from? What was a Daisy, a service team, age-level training, *Safety-Wise*? I seemed to be the outsider, the only clueless person in a room full of tuned-in veterans.

New leader training cleared the most glaring discrepancies, but I was still left with a feeling of impending disaster as our first meeting approached.

How would I be able to:

• Effectively run a meeting and teach **anything** without losing my grip on sanity?

• Keep track of all this paperwork?

• Make sure everything that needed to go home did?

After much stewing I came up with three things that have made the mechanics of being a leader a relative breeze.

1. Getting Organized

The first brainstorm I came up with was our troop notebook. I bought a three-ring binder and a pack of dividers. The first section I labeled "Meeting Notes," and we'll talk about this later. The next section was "Individual Records." I completed an "Individual Girl's Record" form for each girl and put them in alphabetical order. I then started a "Brownie Try-It Worksheet" for each girl and placed it with her individual record. I updated these sheets after each meeting or trip.

The next divider was for "Leader Handbooks." This is where I keep our copy of the *Blue Book of Basic Documents* and *Safety-Wise*. The next section is "Financial Records." The "Detailed Cash Record" is found here and I update it when I spend or receive troop money. This makes the end-of-the-year report a whole lot simpler than it could be.

The last section was labeled "Letters Home" and is for a copy of each correspondence sent to a girl's home. I bought a zippered pencil holder and put it in the front of the notebook for the loose change and receipts. I typed a list of the girls' names, addresses, and phone numbers, and their parents' names, and put it right behind the pencil holder. I was off and running.

2. Knowing What to Expect

The second idea was for a standard meeting format. My experience as a mom had taught me my kids do better when they know what to expect. With this in mind I developed an outline for our meetings that has been in place since meeting number one. All I do is change the story, program activities, and announcements from one month to the next. I print a copy of our meeting agenda for each month and use it to keep the meeting running on schedule. Then, after the meeting, I file it in the "Meeting Notes" section of the notebook. This way I can always look back and see what we've done in previous months.

Ours is an after-school troop, but I still save the snack for the end of the meeting or nothing else would get done. I read the girls a story during snack time. Cleanup and other duties are assigned via a kaper chart (an old term I'd forgotten over the years).

3. Keep Proper Files

The last idea was for a troop file box. Besides all the things you'd expect to find, like files for training, catalogs, and various field trips, each girl has her own file folder. I also have a file folder. An emergency information card is taped inside each girl's folder that gives both mom and dad's work number, whom to contact in case of an emergency and how to contact her or him, who can pick up the girl, and any other relevant information. All items and correspondences to go home are filed; one copy is placed in each girl's folder. It is each girl's responsibility to check her folder at the end of the meetings for stuff to go home.

This has worked out remarkably well. I don't have to worry about catching the parents to give them information at the end of the meetings. Also, parents have learned to put any notes or messages for me in my folder so I don't forget what they've told me while I'm talking to three people at a time. Checks for field trips also go in my folder and I keep a stash of small envelopes in the file box for cash payments. The parent paying cash seals the money in the envelope and writes her daughter's name on the envelope before stuffing it in my folder. I never have to wonder where the money in my pocket came from or who hasn't paid for what.

Over the last two years I've been contacted by several other leaders who had heard our meetings are well organized and wanted to know how that has happened. I've always passed along these tips with one very important caveat: **stay flexible**. Meeting disasters happen no matter how organized you are. Just don't be so set on your meeting goals that your outline becomes more important than having fun.

Libby Marks McDonell

Libby Marks McDonell

Pre-Meeting

Sign in on attendance board ✓

Find job on kaper chart ✓

Start-up activity ✓

Opening

Friendship circle ✓

Girl Scout Promise ✓

Song ✓

Announcements and Planning for Future Meetings

Program Activities ✓

Cleanup ✓

Snack

Brownie story time ✓

Snack cleanup ✓

Closing

Friendship circle ✓

Song ✓

Friendship squeeze ✓

Pick up folder information before leaving ✓

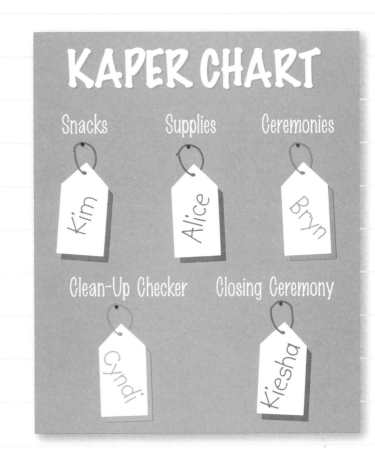

The Progression of Trips

Trips should be planned progressively—that is, first trips should be simple and close to home, with subsequent trips longer in duration and farther in distance. Be sure to use *Safety-Wise* for guidance on a whole range of important considerations, like proper adult-to-girl ratios, travel and transportation safety, and camping or lodging.

MEETING-TIME TRIPS

Girls visit points of interest in the neighborhood: for example, a walk to a nearby garden or park, or a short ride by car or public transportation to visit a civic building, such as a firehouse or courthouse.

DAY TRIPS

These are daytime excursions away from the regular troop meeting place and time. Girls might plan an all-day visit to a historic landmark or building and include a bag lunch or plan a meal in a restaurant. Another possibility is for the girls to attend a Girl Scout council-sponsored or Girl Scout neighborhood-sponsored event.

SIMPLE OVERNIGHT TRIPS

These usually involve one or two nights away. The destination might be a nearby state or national park, a Girl Scout camp, a historic site, or local attraction. The group may stay in a hostel, hotel, motel, or on campgrounds.

It Could
Happen to You

Hypothetical Scenarios and Tips for Dealing with Them

During your tenure as a Girl Scout leader there are bound to be a few sticky situations or times when you will have to deal with a difficult child or parent. The scenarios below are all fictitious, but they could potentially happen to any leader at any time.

After reading each incident, consider the tips offered for handling it. What else would you do? Who in your council would you call for guidance if you were really unsure about a solution to a particularly sensitive or trying problem?

The attendance in your troop has been steadily declining. You started the year with 25 girls and now you never have more than 10 girls at a meeting. After the latest meeting, you ask two of the girls if they know why fewer girls have been coming. One mumbles something about "only doing crafts stuff" and runs to her waiting father. You have been doing the activities the girls have chosen themselves, and so you are a bit surprised by this answer.

 for Leaders

- The Girl Scout program offers a wide array of activities on any number of topics. You can guide the girls in your troop or group to sample new kinds of activities, or try variations on their favorites. As the leader, you may offer a new activity for all to try.

- Peer pressure can have a tremendous impact on children, even those as young as Brownie Girl Scouts. Be alert to situations where the girls may be reluctant to let their true feelings show. For example, voting publicly on what kinds of activities to do, some girls may not be expressing their true desires; instead, they may be voting the same way as their friends.

- Attrition in your troop may be due to a large number of factors, so hear the opinions of the children as something to be explored. Contact the parents of the girls who have ceased coming to find out why they are no longer involved.

Jenny is very active. She never seems to sit still and she talks all the time. Some girls in your troop would like to attend a ballet that is only in town for a limited engagement. You know that some of the children are mature enough and would behave and enjoy a performance. Others, like Jenny, would probably make your life miserable, and they might disturb other people at the theater.

TiPS for Leaders

- If you encounter recurrent behavior problems, ask to meet with the parents or guardians of the child. You might discover that there are underlying reasons for the girl's behavior—for example, a learning disability that prevents her from sitting still for too long. Her parents or guardians can advise you on the best way to deal with the child.

- In a special setting like a theater, one-on-one supervision might be required. To prevent the child from feeling bad or different, you might ask a group of Cadette or Senior Girl Scouts to attend the show with you, making sure that one of the more mature Girl Scouts spends time with the potentially disruptive child.

- Establish the expected behavior before your trip. Make sure that each girl understands and can repeat what will be expected of her. Also, if privileges will be revoked due to inappropriate behavior, make sure that the girls know this in advance.

You have never gone camping and hate to consider waking up without access to a blow dryer and an indoor bathroom! Some of the girls in your troop have been lobbying for a camping trip. You can't put them off any longer. What can you do?

TiPS for Leaders

- Now is the time to enlist the support of the girls' parents or guardians. If you ask, you will probably find that some of the girls who want to go camping have done so already with their families. Ask mothers or guardians familiar with camping to come along on the trip, and you may have more fun than you expect.

- Choose a campsite that is not too rustic. In many places you can find platform tents complete with cots. In these places, you might also find bathrooms or wash houses that feature amenities like running water, both hot and cold, and electrical outlets for your hair dryer.

- You can also discuss this dilemma with staff at your council. They might know of another troop that would not mind having a few additional girls for a camping adventure.

You love to camp. You started as a Girl Scout and nowadays you still spend your vacations in the outdoors. You are eager to pass along your love of nature to the girls in your troop. They either yawn or tell you how much they hate bugs!

TiPS for Leaders

- Girls should not be forced to do activities that they do not like. But if they are vetoing certain kinds of things simply because they are unfamiliar, there are several approaches that you can take. Ask them the reasons they don't want to do something. You may discover misconceptions—for example, it's uncomfortable or dirty—that you can dispel. Find opportunities to broaden horizons. If girls hate bugs, explore ways that encounters can be kept to a minimum. Investigate different kinds of bugs, butterflies, and fireflies. You may also uncover hidden reasons. One girl may be afraid to be away from home. In that case, a conversation with parents may be important.

- If girls don't seem ready to go on a complete overnight camping trip, start smaller. Take them on a day hike that will provide them with an opportunity to learn more about nature. If possible, show them places where people camp and the ways that people cook when they are spending time outdoors.

You started with one Try-It. Now that's all the girls want to do. They love getting the triangles and spend a lot of time plotting which Try-Its are the easiest and quickest to earn so they can fill up their sashes and vests. They seem happy, but you're not sure about this relentless pursuit of triangles!

TiPS for Leaders

- The Girl Scout program offers variety. Some activities lead to an award and many do not. If the girls in your troop seem more interested in the physical Try-It rather than the actual experience of doing the activities, then it may be time to take a break and do something else. Brainstorm ideas with the girls. Present additional possibilities by introducing them to some of the other Girl Scout resources on pages 55–57 of this book. This may be the time to plan a trip or a troop service project.

- For some children Girl Scouting affords a new place—maybe the first place—to feel successful. A sense of accomplishment can mean enhanced self-esteem or a way to break the barrier of shyness. The single-minded pursuit of triangles, therefore, may not be entirely negative, but a balanced approach to the Girl Scout program will enrich girls' experiences.

- Plan award ceremonies when Try-Its are distributed. This way you can pace the awarding of Try-Its.

You are the leader of a Brownie Girl Scout troop that meets in a local church. All the girls in the troop are of Hispanic origin, mostly with Puerto Rican and Dominican backgrounds. The community is also composed of Asians—people with Korean and Taiwanese backgrounds—and some recently arrived Russian Jewish immigrants. You have heard a few of the girls use ethnic slurs, obviously imitating words they have heard at home, on the street, on television, or somewhere outside the troop setting.

 for Leaders

- This is a very sensitive situation. Chances are that the girls do not even understand the insults they are slinging. Also, if girls are indeed learning these slurs at home, they may not comprehend why they are inappropriate. Use the *Connections* booklet, which is a part of the Issues for Girl Scouts series, as a learning tool. As girls read the information and do the activities, they will begin to appreciate differences in people that range from external appearances to cultural norms.

- Use this as an opportunity to explain that everyone has a unique background, and often with a blend of different ethnicities. Show the girls that, even though most of them speak Spanish at home, they too have many differences. Have girls learn about their own families' backgrounds. Use what they learn in a discussion of different cultures. Include in your discussion the differences between Puerto Rico and the Dominican Republic.

- Make sure that girls understand that ethnic slurs will not be tolerated at Girl Scout meetings or events. Have them repeat the Promise and Law as an affirmation that they will appreciate others.

One of the girls in your troop has informed you that her mother will not let her participate in the Girl Scout Cookie Sale this year. Two other girls overhear her and say that if she doesn't sell Girl Scout cookies, she shouldn't go on troop trips.

- Girls are not required to sell Girl Scout Cookies. Therefore, this should never be a condition for participation in other activities. If a parent or guardian does not want her daughter to sell cookies, perhaps there is another role that the girl can play. For example, maybe she can help sort or distribute the cookie boxes. Or maybe she can help to make fliers or posters relating to the Girl Scout Cookie Sale.

- Explain to all the girls that each member of the troop contributes in her own way. If someone can't participate in the cookie sale, maybe she can take an important role in other ways to support the troop. The girl herself may have ideas on how she can contribute.

Activities "in a Pinch"

Despite all your hard work, some plans may go awry at the very last minute. The activities in this section are intended to help fill in the gaps when this happens. Generally, they require few materials and little preparation time. The activities have been categorized according to the chapters in the girls' handbook to facilitate your planning.

A Survival Kit for Brownie Girl Scout Leaders

Although succeeding as a Brownie Girl Scout leader requires any number of intangibles—for example, a sense of humor, patience, and loads of caring—there are some tangible items that will make your experience more relaxed and enjoyable.

The following is a list of items that can be included in a "Survival Kit" for Brownie Girl Scout leaders:

- A basic first-aid kit. (See *Safety-Wise*.)
- Crayons, markers, colored pencils.
- Construction paper, ruled paper, index cards.
- String, ribbons, cardboard, postcards, used greeting cards, and other collage materials.
- Age-appropriate books and magazines.
- Balls.
- Jump ropes.
- Board games.

If you keep this kit handy during meetings, girls who complete activities early can start something new rather than just sitting around idly. Also, if an activity falls through at the last minute, you will be able to create a new one using the materials in your kit.

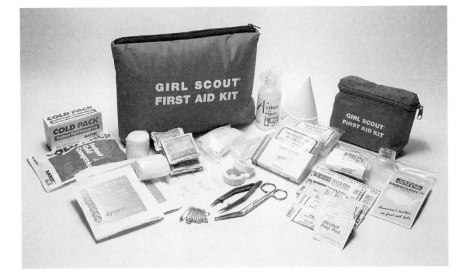

Brownie Girl Scouts, Let's Get Started!

ACTIVITY ONE: ACT IT OUT

The girls will love acting out the Brownie story.

Preparation Tips:

None

Preparation Time:

None

Materials:

Copies of the *Brownie Girl Scout Handbook.*

Directions:

1. Girls can act out "The Brownie story" on pages 29–32 of the *Brownie Girl Scout Handbook* in a number of different ways. Help them decide how to begin.

2. Facilitate the process by ensuring that all girls are involved and get to play the roles of their choosing. You may want to do the activity several times in different ways to accommodate the desires of all the members of your troop or group.

ACTIVITY TWO: PASS IT ON

Girls enjoy making their own special traditions. Help them create their own version of the friendship squeeze, a Girl Scout favorite.

Preparation Tips:

The girls will need to know how to do the friendship squeeze. If they haven't learned this Girl Scout tradition yet, now's a great time to teach it to them.

Materials:

None.

Directions:

1. Have girls do the traditional friendship squeeze, which is described on page 19 of the *Brownie Girl Scout Handbook.*

2. Brainstorm different ways to execute the friendship squeeze. For example, each girl might give a compliment to the girl whose hand she is squeezing.

3. Try some of these ideas out as you continue to stand in the circle.

4. Discuss how this popular Girl Scout tradition could be adapted to accommodate girls with disabilities that may prevent them from doing it the original way.

ACTIVITY THREE: SAVING WITH STYLE

Your Girl Scout troop or group may have items that need storage—permission slips, activity cards, pencils, crayons, and other supplies. In addition, the troop or group may need a place to hold money earned from the Girl Scout Cookie Sale. Make this special decoupage box as a place to keep troop supplies.

Preparation Tips:

Collect magazines and pictures in order to do this project. Use common white glue or make a trip to a craft store for special decoupage glue.

Preparation Time:

Variable, depending on the materials that you already have available.

Materials:

- Boxes. Shoe boxes work particularly well. The girls can share one box, or each girl can work on her own box.
- Magazines and cards for pictures.
- A pair of scissors for each girl.
- Glue or decoupage glue.

Directions:

1. Have girls cut out lots of pictures from the magazines.

2. Once they feel they have enough pictures, girls can begin to glue them onto the box or boxes. To create a collage, the pictures should overlap.

3. When the box or boxes are covered and the girls are satisfied with their work, they can protect it by brushing on a coat of white glue or by using decoupage glue. If they use decoupage glue, they will need to follow the directions on the specific product.

4. To make things fancier, girls can line the bottom and the inside of their box or boxes with felt.

Taking Care of Yourself

Brownie Girl Scouts may not know the term *self-esteem*, but they sure do know how good it feels to be praised and given lots of positive attention. Help the girls in your troop feel good about themselves with the following activity.

Note:

If you do not have access to a television or a video recorder at your meeting place, this activity can be done by reading girls a story from a book.

Preparation Tips:

Discussion is fundamental to this activity. Use a video that you have already seen or preview the one that you select. Help girls to recognize different traits in the fictitious characters that they see in the video, and then to see how some of these attributes apply to themselves and the other girls in the troop.

Preparation Time:

The time that it takes to watch the video if you have never seen it before.

Materials:

• An age-appropriate video, preferably with one or more strong female characters who have easily identifiable traits.
• VCR.
• TV set.

Directions:

1. Have girls view the video, either in its entirety or a part that you find particularly significant.

2. After the video is finished, each girl can describe positive traits she has observed in the characters.

3. Discuss with the girls the kinds of traits that they have ascribed to the characters. Help them see why these attributes are positive not only for the characters but for people in general.

4. Have the girls sit in a circle. Ask each girl to name two positive characteristics of the girl on her right. Explain that they can use the traits that you discussed earlier, or any other ones, as long as they are positive.

Many kids like to cook and even more like to eat, so enjoy a quick "salsa fest" with your troop.

Preparation Tips:

To do this activity you will probably have to make a quick trip to the grocery store to buy the ingredients. Aside from that, there is no other preparation necessary.

Preparation Time:

Depending on the grocery checker, 15-20 minutes.

Materials:

- 1 pound of tomatoes (can be fresh or canned).
- 1 small onion.
- 1 tablespoon of lime juice (use a fresh lime or bottled juice).
- 2 tablespoons of chopped fresh coriander or cilantro, if desired. (1 teaspoon of dried coriander or cilantro may be substituted.)
- Tortilla chips.
- Cutting board(s) and knives appropriate for use by girls.
- Book with a story about a girl from Mexico (optional).

Directions:

1. Have girls prepare and measure all the ingredients. If the girls themselves chop the tomatoes, be sure to supervise them as they use the knives.

2. Once the ingredients are ready, they can all be combined, in no particular order, in a bowl.

3. Allow the salsa to stand for 30 minutes. During this time you can have the girls clean up.

4. Taste your creation. After the girls have eaten, you might choose to read them a story about a girl in Mexico. Or you might just discuss foods and the different places that popular dishes come from.

Note:

For variety, you can also add other vegetables including corn, carrots, or celery.

Many adults appreciate the benefits of yoga after they have had a particularly stressful or hectic day. Girls, too, can enjoy the calming effects of this ancient form of exercise. Try these activities and see if you and the girls can make it all the way through without bursting into fits of laughter.

Preparation Tips:

To use this activity successfully, you should acquaint yourself with the exercises so that you can show girls how to do them with relative ease.

Preparation Time:

5-10 minutes

Materials:

No materials are really needed. Comfortable clothing would be useful.

Directions:

1. Keeping your shoulders stationary, your mouth closed, and teeth together, exhale and thrust your chin and head as far forward as can be done comfortably. As you inhale, slowly come back to the center; then tuck your chin into your neck, forcing an extreme double chin. Exhale and relax as you return to the center position.

2. While sitting in a chair, push your shoulders forward, exhale, and thrust your chin and head as far forward as comfortable. At the same time, open your mouth wide and stretch your tongue out trying to touch your chin. Simultaneously, place your hands on your knees. With your arms straight and your fingers widely spread, push on your hands, so that you feel it in your arms and shoulders. Your eyes should be focused on a point straight ahead. Your whole body should be stretched. Hold your breath while briefly maintaining this position. Sit back, inhale, and relax. Repeat if you desire.

Because germs cannot be seen, it is sometimes hard for youngsters to understand what they are or how they travel. Use this very simple activity to reinforce the importance of washing hands in the fight against germs.

Preparation Tips and Time:

No preparation is really necessary.

Materials:

- Soap.
- Water.
- Paper towels.
- Glitter.

Directions:

1. Conduct a short discussion about germs, including information about what they are and how they spread. See page 50 in the *Brownie Girl Scout Handbook.*

2. To portray these concepts visually, place glitter on the hand of one of the girls. Have her shake hands with the next girl. This continues until everyone has had a chance to shake hands with the girl next to her.

3. Discuss the results. Explain to the girls that the glitter represents germs, and that, as the hands touched one another, the germs spread. The cleaner someone's hands are kept, therefore, the fewer germs will be transferred from one person to another.

4. Have the girls wash the glitter from their hands.

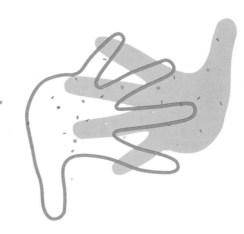

Family and Friends

ACTIVITY ONE: BROWNIE GIRL SCOUT POSTCARDS

Girls can make and send postcards from their Brownie Girl Scout meeting. In this way the whole family can keep up with the girls' activities and adventures.

Preparation Tips and Time:

None needed.

Materials:

- 5" x 8" index cards.
- Crayons, pencils, or markers.
- Stamps.

Directions:

1. The girls decorate one side of the cards. They can write descriptions of things they do at Brownie Girl Scout meetings. They can also draw pictures of them, or of anything that means "Brownie Girl Scouting" to them—their Brownie Girl Scout pin, their Girl Scout pin, their troop number, a patch, etc.

2. Ask the girls to turn the index cards over and to hold them horizontally. Next, have them draw a line down the middle (or fold the cards in half and draw a line down the crease). The right-hand side is for the name and address of the person to whom each girl will be sending her card. The cards can be sent to parents, grandparents, friends from camp or school, siblings, cousins, etc.

3. On the left-hand side, the girls can write a short note about their Brownie Girl Scout activities.

4. Put stamps on the postcards. Be sure to check the names and addresses before mailing them.

Help your Brownie Girl Scouts celebrate the connections among family members or friends by making links in a chain.

Preparation Tips and Time:

None needed.

Materials:

- Construction paper in different colors.
- Scissors.
- Tape.
- Pencils or markers.

Directions:

1. Have the girls cut the paper into strips.
2. Each strip stands for a friend or a member of a girl's family. Have each girl write that person's name on one side of the strip of paper.
3. Next to the name, girls should write a word that describes what they like about that person.
4. Tape the two ends of the strip together. Connect another "link" to this one by threading it through the first link and taping its ends together.
5. The girls can share their chains with their families or friends. Or use them to decorate the Girl Scout meeting place for a party.

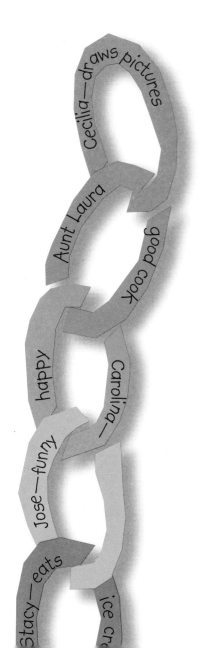

ACTIVITY THREE: WHAT DO THEY DO?

Girls of all ages are interested in what people really do when they are at work. This activity is an easy way for the girls to "try on" a number of different careers. It will also help them decide which ones they want to learn more about.

Preparation Tips and Time:

Ask girls to bring in an assortment of props. Encourage them to use their imagination. For example, a lunch box can serve as a doctor's kit, a tool chest for a plumber, or a cash register.

Materials:

- Paper.
- Pen.
- Props.

Directions:

1. As a group, the girls list the work experience of the people in their families—parents, aunts, uncles, grandparents, etc.
2. In pairs or small groups, girls act out what they think each of those jobs is like. For example:
   - If a parent is a teacher, the girls act out the role of the students as well as the role of the teacher.
   - If an aunt is a salesperson, one girl acts out her role while other girls play the customers and the cashier.
3. Once they have acted out a couple of different careers, find out which they like best and why. Would they like to find out more about one of these fields? Follow up at a later meeting with a trip to a workplace.

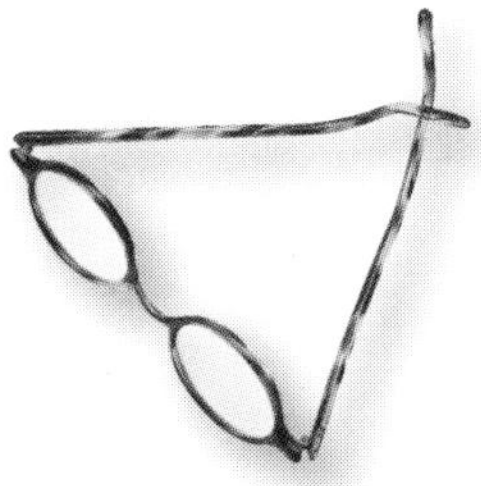

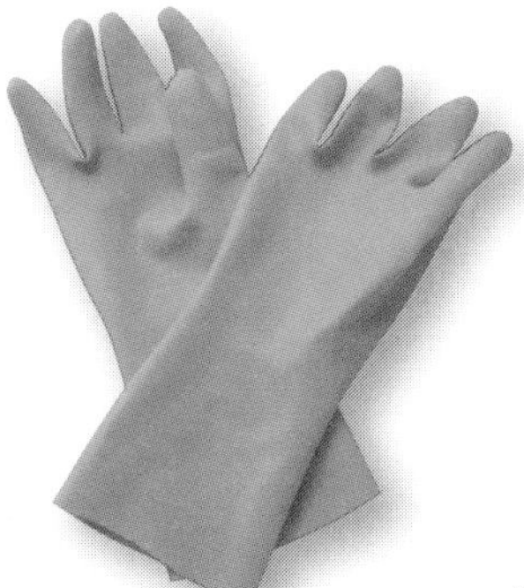

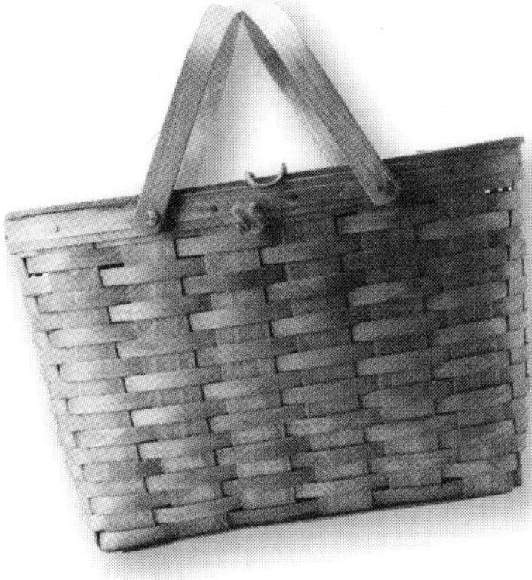

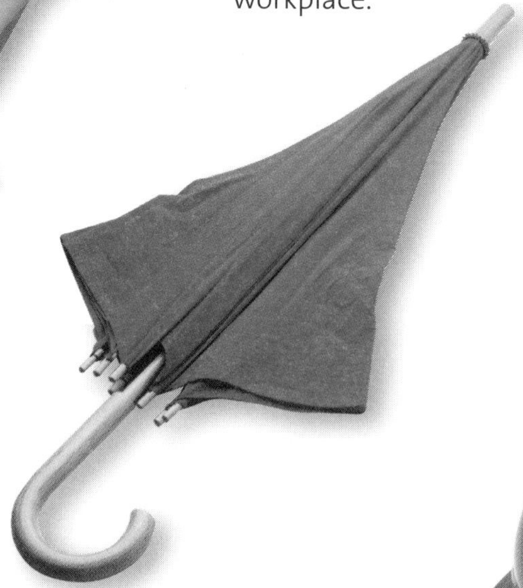

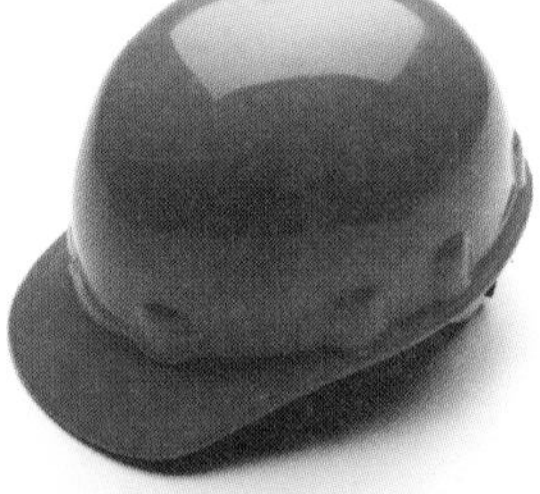

What's Out There?

Bugs can be fascinating, and girls can learn a lot from them, too. Take the girls in your troop on a "bug safari" and see for yourself!

Preparation Tips:

You can ask each girl to bring her own jar, but you should also have a few jars on hand in case some girls forget. Girls can also work in pairs if not enough jars are available.

Bug is the common term for a whole slew of creeping, crawling, and flying creatures. If it has six legs, it's an insect. But insects also go through other stages of growth when they look completely different. For example, butterflies were once caterpillars. Before you start, find out about stinging, biting, or poisonous critters to avoid.

Preparation Time:

It will take about 30 minutes to punch holes in the lids of the jars.

Materials:

- One plastic or glass jar, with tiny holes punched in the lid, for each girl in the troop.
- Magnifying glass (one or more can be shared if they are available).
- Drawing paper, crayons, pens, markers.

Directions:

1. Have girls find a bug. Some good places to look are outside the Girl Scout meeting place, in the grass, in the cracks in the sidewalk, or on a tree.

2. Bring the bugs back to the meeting place or another place where girls can take time to inspect what they have captured. Together, look at the bugs closely and consider the following questions:

   - How many body parts does it have? (Insects have three, while spiders have two.)
   - Does it have long skinny feelers *(antennae)* on the top of its head?
   - Does it have six legs? Whereas insects have six legs, spiders have eight legs. Centipedes and millipedes, of course, have many more legs.

3. Now have the girls look at their bugs even more closely. Does the outer covering look hard or soft? How would a hard outer covering help with survival? Using the magnifying lens, have them look at the mouth parts. Does the bug look as if it chews its food with its pointy jaws, or does it have a straw-like mouth? Can the girls think of a reason why these creatures are an important part of a habitat?

4. If time permits and girls are still showing interest, have them draw pictures of their creatures.

5. Most importantly, have the girls release their captives outside.

Each type of frog makes an identifying sound. Frogs respond to sounds made by their own kind. Here are the names of three types of frogs and the special sound that each one makes:

Bullfrog—RI-BBIT

Spring peeper--PEEP-PEEP

Chorus frog—WRAANK

Preparation Tips:

None.

Preparation Time:

About 20 minutes to write the names of each type of frog and its sound on separate index cards or slips of paper.

Materials:

- A bandanna or piece of cloth for a blindfold.

- Slips of paper or small index cards with the names of each type of frog and the sound it makes. Each girl should get one, so you will have to write the frog names and sounds more than once.

- A hat or bag in which to place the index cards or slips of paper so girls can choose one without seeing it first.

Directions:

1. Have each girl pull out an index card or slip of paper from the hat. She should keep secret what she reads.

2. Simulate a pond by having all the girls in your troop stand in a circle and imagine that they are a small body of water.

3. Ask one girl to volunteer to begin the game by being blindfolded.

4. After she is blindfolded, have the other girls in the group begin to make the frog sounds that they have chosen. The blindfolded girl must find and tag someone who is making the same sound as was written on her paper.

Make sure that each girl has a chance to be blindfolded.

Make a special zoo of endangered animals with your troop.

Girls can pick an endangered animal from the following list or choose their own:

Florida panther.   Peregrine falcon.   Siberian tiger.

Black-footed ferret.   West Indian manatee.   Giant panda.

African elephant.

Preparation Tips:

Before you do this activity, you may need to borrow some books from the library that the girls can use as references.

Preparation Time:

Start to collect magazines from friends and neighbors a few months before.

Materials:

- Old magazines with pictures of wildlife and the outdoors.
- Large sheets of plain, heavy paper.
- Markers and crayons.
- Information about endangered species.

Directions:

1. Spend some time talking about endangered animals. Help girls understand the difference between *endangered* and *extinct*. Explain to them the rules and laws that are made to protect these animals.

2. Using the large sheets of paper, have each girl create a poster "habitat" for the animal that she has chosen. As they work, discuss with them the things the animals might need to have in the environment—sources of food, light, water, shelter, or other animals, for example. Help them include these things in their works.

3. Place all the completed posters together. Have the girls imagine they are visiting a zoo or a wildlife preserve.

4. If time permits, or at the beginning of the next meeting, have each girl describe her animal—why it is endangered, where it lives, and any other pertinent information she chooses to share.

People Near and Far

This is a variation of a game from Girl Guides of New Zealand. It encourages girls to find visual images that reflect important Girl Scout messages, awards, or projects.

Preparation Tips: Here are some possible messages that Brownie Girl Scouts would be acquainted with:

Messages from the Girl Scout Promise and Law

1. A Girl Scout serves God and her country.
2. A Girl Scout is friendly and helpful.
3. A Girl Scout respects authority.
4. A Girl Scout uses resources wisely.

Names of Try-Its

1. Dancercize
2. Listening to the Past
3. Science in Action
4. Earth and Sky

Projects

1. Girls Are Great!
2. *GirlSports*
3. Read to Lead

On separate sheets of paper, write messages or phrases for each pair of girls.

Preparation Time: Five to ten minutes.

Materials:

• Enough magazines and newspapers for each group to look through for pictures.

• Scissors for each group.

• Cardboard, construction paper, or even plain white paper to display pictures.

• Glue.

Directions:

1. Divide girls into pairs. Give each pair a slip of paper with a message on it.
2. Each pair finds pictures that represent the message. For example, "A Girl Scout is friendly and helpful" can be represented by a picture of a girl carrying groceries for a neighbor. The Dancercize Try-It can be represented by a girl or group of girls dancing, or by a collage of ballet slippers, musical notes, and instruments.
3. Each pair displays its picture and the other girls guess what message it represents.

ACTIVITY TWO: DARA—A GAME FROM AFRICA

This game is like checkers, but you can't jump over your partner's pieces. It's also like tic-tac-toe, because you have to get three of your pieces in a row.

Preparation Tips:

Girls should play this game in pairs. They can scratch out a game board on a smooth patch of earth, or draw with chalk on the sidewalk. Or you can draw it on paper and make copies. The game board is a grid of five by six squares lined up. Gather enough counters so that each player has 12 pieces; these can be pebbles or beans.

Preparation Time:

Five to ten minutes.

Materials:

- Copies of the game board (the grid).

- Twelve pebbles for each girl. The pebbles should be small enough to fit inside the squares on the grid.

Directions:

1. Each girl places her 12 pieces in the squares on the playing grid. Initially, each girl cannot have more than two playing pieces in adjacent squares.

2. Girls take turns moving their playing pieces one space at a time. They can move in any direction, including diagonally. Remind the girls that jumping is not allowed.

3. The goal is to place three pieces in a vertical or horizontal row, as shown. When this is accomplished, a girl may remove one of her opponent's pieces.

4. The game is over when one girl is no longer able to line up three playing pieces, or when all of a girl's game pieces have been used.

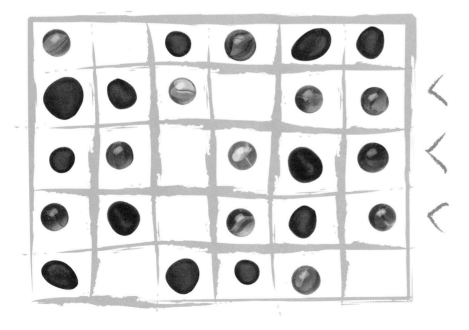

Technology can be defined as the application of science to make life easier. From eyeglasses to computers, from vitamins to cell phones, we come into contact with technology each and every day. Help girls start thinking of science and technology as important parts of their lives.

Preparation Tips and Time:

Photocopy the chart on page 54, or make your own. Each team of girls will need one chart. Have on hand different examples of technology—for example, a hair dryer, a watch, a bottle of vitamins, and a computer game. Note that you can use this activity at home, at school, in the neighborhood, while traveling, or at camp.

Materials:

- The chart on page 54.
- Pencils.
- Clipboards (optional).

Directions:

1. Introduce the concept of technology both verbally and visually, if possible. Have the girls give other examples. Explain that girls will form teams of two to find technology at work. Emphasize that girls should remain in pairs. Encourage girls to find more than one example for each category listed on the chart. Before the girls start, clearly outline the search boundaries. Establish a signal to indicate a start and stop time and choose a place for gathering at the end of the search.

2. Allow enough time for girls to fully cover the area they are searching, whether a room, house, or camp.

3. Reserve time to discuss the activity. Let girls share their "finds" and explain why they chose to put certain items in particular categories. You might ask questions like the following: What was the most unusual thing your team found? What was the hardest thing to find? What was the easiest? Ask girls what technologies are the most important to them.

Some possible answers:

Counting or Measuring
calculator
cash register
coffee maker
traffic counter

Using Memory or Programs
computer
microwave
VCR
CD player

Turning Things On and Off
light switch
water faucet
car key
radio dial

Sensing Change
thermostat
automatic doors
smoke detector
sprinkler system

Holding Things Together
nails
glue
thread
buttons
snaps

Changing One Thing to Another
microwave
ice machine
lamp
TV set

Making Things Change Size
trash compactor
camera
eyeglasses
popcorn maker

Moving Things
elevator
fan
wheelchair

Making Life Easier
flush toilet
dishwasher
telephone
hair dryer

Can you find examples of technology (science at work)?

Draw or list your observations in each square.

Counting or Measuring	Sensing Change	Making Things Change Size
Using Memory or Programs	Holding Things	Moving Things
Turning Things On and Off	Changing One Thing to Another	Making Life Easier

Resources for Brownie Girl Scouts

Annotated List of Girl Scout Resources for Brownie Girl Scouts

The Girl Scout program is always evolving to meet the needs of girls in contemporary society. Each year Girl Scouts of the USA begins new collaborations with external organizations that have expertise and resources which enrich or expand existing projects and initiatives or which enable entirely new ones to be created. Although new materials are always being developed, a number of fundamental publications and resources can be used to support the program goals and overall purpose of Girl Scouting. These resources are listed below.

BROWNIE GIRL SCOUT HANDBOOK

This book provides the foundation for the Girl Scout program for six- to eight-year-olds. Included in its pages are activities, the Girl Scout Promise and Law, Girl Scout history and traditions, safety tips, and many other fun facts, tips, and topics.

TRY-ITS FOR BROWNIE GIRL SCOUTS

Many youngsters agree that earning Try-Its is one of the best parts of being a Brownie Girl Scout. This book includes all the information needed to help girls earn the awards, which they can then wear on their vests or sashes.

ISSUES FOR GIRL SCOUTS

Follow the Reader Book for Brownie Girl Scouts/Aventuras en Lectura para Brownie Girl Scouts

Based on the five objectives of the White House literacy initiative *No Child Left Behind*: phonemic awareness, phonics, fluency, vocabulary and comprehension. This family-centered book is completely bilingual. It addresses an important need for Girl Scout materials in English as well as Spanish and offers families the opportunity to read together using the language in which they feel most comfortable.

New Address...New Friends: Let's Get Movin' Booklet for Brownie/Junior Girl Scouts

Specifically written to help young children express their feelings about a move, become involved in the process and learn about their new city or country. Filled with fun activities, exercises and safety tips designed to take the apprehension out of moving.

And check out the Junior Girl Scout Badges that are posted on Girl Scout Central www.girlscouts.org/program/gs_central/

FUN AND EASY ACTIVITIES—

Fun and Easy Nature and Science Investigations
Investigaciones divertidas y fáciles de la naturaleza y la ciencia

This booklet contains activities and worksheets that any leader anywhere can use to guide girls through their own science and nature explorations. No special equipment required. English and Spanish versions.

Fun and Easy Activities—Nature and Science/Actividades divertidas y fáciles— Naturaleza y ciencia

This activity book uses adventure, self-expression, and whimsy to help Brownie and Junior Girl Scouts explore nature on their own or with the family. Also a great source of troop and group pre-activities. Bilingual (English and Spanish).

GIRL SCOUTS AGAINST SMOKING:

Daisy and Brownie Girl Scouts

The dangers of smoking are undeniable and this pamphlet addresses them through accurate information and engaging activities.

IN THE ZONE

Living Drug Free series provides girls with a framework of solid substance abuse facts and information. Age-appropriate activities are designed to teach and reinforce positive, empowering messages about living drug free. Activities that emphasize learning by doing are at the heart of the *In The Zone* series.

GAMES FOR GIRL SCOUTS

Playing games is as much a part of Brownie Girl Scouting as any other activity. This book will give you, as a Girl Scout leader, tons of ideas for games that you may remember from your childhood as well as variations on them and completely new ones.

LET'S CELEBRATE

Sometimes, when planning a ceremony, you need a spark of inspiration or an answer to a question of etiquette. *Let's Celebrate* will provide the answers.

TREFOIL AROUND THE WORLD

Girl Scouting in foreign countries can be fascinating in both its similarities and differences to what is done in the United States. *Trefoil Around the World* provides insights into Girl Scout organizations in all the WAGGGS countries.

GIRL SCOUTS GO GLOBAL!

With the world more interconnected than ever before, it is important for girls to have a firm understanding and appreciation of other cultures. *Go Global!* provides just the information and activities that will help to fulfill this goal. This publication combines bright, flashy graphics with great activities to win the interest of girls and adults alike.

Additional Resources

The list below offers a sampling of high-quality materials that support and enhance the content of resources produced by Girl Scouts of the USA. These books are categorized according to the topics as they appear in the *Brownie Girl Scout Handbook*.

Chapter 1: Brownie Girl Scouts, Let's Get Started!

Angell, Carole S. *Celebrations Around the World: A Multicultural Handbook*. Golden, Colo.: Fulcrum Publishing, 1996.

Brown, Fern G. *Daisy and the Girl Scouts: The Story of Juliette Gordon Low*. Morton Grove: Albert Whitman & Company, 1996.

Delisle, Jim, and Deb Delisle. *Growing Good Kids: 28 Original Activities that Promote Self-Awareness, Compassion, and Leadership*. Minneapolis, Minn.: Free Spirit Publishing, 1997.

Orlando, Louise. *The Multicultural Game Book: More Than 70 Traditional Games from 30 Countries/Grades 1-6*. New York: Scholastic Press, 1995.

Chapter 2: Taking Care of Yourself

Cohen-Posey, Kate. *How to Handle Bullies, Teasers and Other Meanies*. Amsterdam, N.Y.: Rainbow Books, 1995.

Eberle, Bob. *Scamper*. Waco, Tex.: Prufrock Press, 1997.

Limpus, Bruce. *Lights! Camera! Action!* Waco, Tex.: Prufrock Press, 1994.

Maguire, Arlene. *We're All Special*. Santa Monica, Calif.: Portunus Publishing, 1998.

Mather, Anne D., and Louise B. Weldon. *The Cat at the Door: And Other Stories to Live By*. Center City, Minn.: Hazelden Information Education, 1991.

Nowicki, Stephen Jr., and Marshall Duke. *Helping the Child Who Doesn't Fit In: Clinical Psychologists Decipher the Hidden Dimensions of Social Rejection*. Atlanta, Ga.: Peachtree Publishers, 1992.

Plantos, Ted. *Heather Hits Her First Home Run*. Buffalo, N.Y.: Black Moss Press, 1989.

TV Smarts for Kids (Video)
This short and entertaining video was created in conjunction with the National Cable Television Association just for youngsters. It shows how important it is to be a critical viewer of television. The video is available from the National Cable Television Association, 1724 Massachusetts Ave., N.W., Washington, D.C. 20036.

Chapter 3: Families and Friends

Bennett, Steve, and Ruth Bennett. *365 TV-Free Activities You Do with Your Child*. Ranier, Wash.: Adams Publishing, 1996.

Gelen, Michael. *The Family Car Songbook: Hundred of Miles of Fun!* Philadelphia, Pa.: Running Press Book Publishers, 1997.

Michelle, Lonnie. *How Kids Make Friends: Secrets for Making Friends, No Matter How Shy You Are*. Evanston, Ill.: Freedom Publishing, 1997.

Running Press Book Publishers. *Family Funbook: More Than 400 Amazing, Amusing, and All-Around Awesome Activities for the Entire Family!* Philadelphia, Pa.: Running Press Book Publishers, 1998.

Chapter 4: What's Out There?

Burton, John, ed., *The Atlas of Endangered Species*. New York: Macmillan Publishing, 1991.

Caldecott, Moyra. *Myths of the Sacred Tree*. Rochester, Vt.: Inner Traditions, 1993.

Chadwick, Douglas. *The Company We Keep: America's Endangered Species*. Washington, D.C.: National Geographic Society, 1997.

Coombes, Allen. *Trees: Eyewitness Handbook*. New York: DK Publishing, 1992.

DeBlieu, Jan. *Meant to Be Wild: The Struggle to Save Endangered Species Through Captive Breeding*. Golden, Colo.: Fulcrum Publishing, 1993.

Dickerson, Mary C. *The Frog Book*. Mineola, N.Y.: Dover, 1969.

Imes, Rick. *The Practical Entomologist*. New York: Fireside, 1992.

National Wildlife Foundation. *Ranger Rick's NatureScope: Trees Are Terrific*. Washington, D.C.: National Wildlife Federation, 1987.

Russo, Monica. *The Insect Almanac: A Year-Round Activity Guide*. New York: Sterling Publishing, 1991.

Stokes, Donald. *A Guide to Observing Insect Lives*. Boston: Little, Brown and Company, 1984.

Tudge, Colin. *Last Animals at the Zoo: How Mass Extinction Can Be Stopped*. Washington, D.C.: Island Press, 1993.

Chapter 5: People Near and Far

Chertok, Bobbi. *Meet The Masterpieces: Learning About Ancient Civilizations Through Art*. New York: Scholastic Press, 1994.

Dineen, Jacqueline, and Nicola Barber. *The World of Art*. Parsippany, N.J.: Silver Burdett Press, a Division of Simon and Schuster, 1998.

Kohl, Maryann, and Jean Potter. *Global Art: Activities, Projects, and Inventions from Around the World*. Beltsville, Md.: Gryphon House, 1998.

Schuman, Jo Miles. *Art from Many Hands*. Worcester, Mass.: Davis Publications, 1981.

Wiseman, Ann. *Making Things: The Handbook of Creative Discovery*. Boston: Little, Brown & Company, 1996.

DRAWING FOR THE
Absolute AND *Utter*
BEGINNER

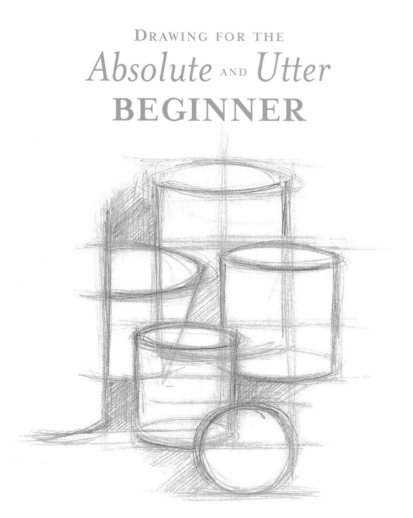

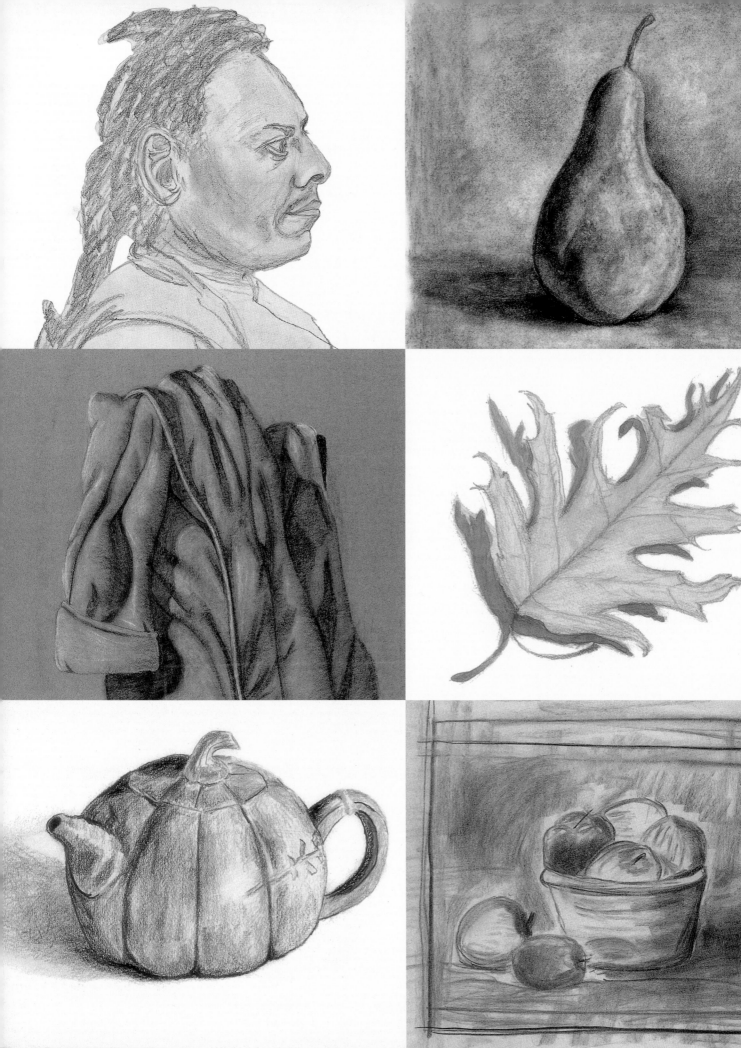

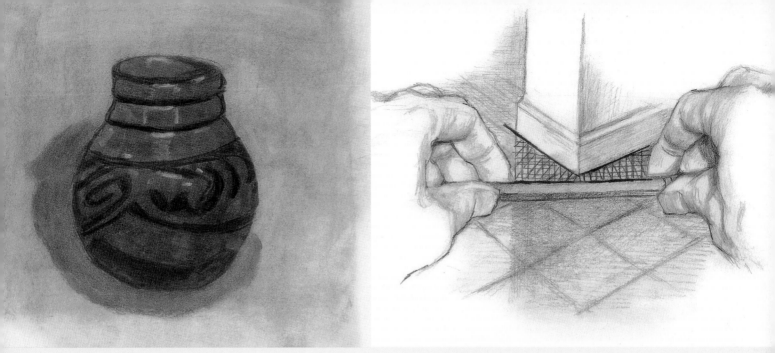

DRAWING FOR THE
Absolute AND *Utter*
BEGINNER

CLAIRE WATSON GARCIA

WATSON-GUPTILL PUBLICATIONS / NEW YORK

Senior Acquisitions Editor, Joy Aquilino
Edited by Robbie Capp
Designed by Areta Buk
Cover designed by Sivan Earnest
Graphic Production by Hector Campbell
Text set in 11-pt. Berthold Garamond

ART CREDITS
Unless otherwise identified, all artwork by the author.
PAGE 1: Drawing by Claire Watson Garcia

PAGE 2: Drawings, top row from left, by student Bob Pingarron, Claire Watson Garcia; center row from left, student Nancy Opgaard, student Linda Fitzgerald; bottom row from left, student Anne Ballantyne, student Kim Nightingale
PAGE 3: Drawings, top row from left, student Jane Wolansky, Claire Watson Garcia; bottom row from left, Claire Watson Garcia, student Anne Ballantyne

PAGE 4: Drawing by student Sherry Artemenko
PAGES 8–9: Drawings, from left, by student Ann Porfilio, Anita St. Marie, student Barbara Kops, student Michelle G. Cappellieri

First published in 2003 in the United States
by Watson-Guptill Publications,
Crown Publishing Group, a division of Random House Inc., New York
www.crownpublishing.com
www.watsonguptill.com

LIBRARY OF CONGRESS CONTROL NUMBER 2003105861
ISBN-13: 978-0-8230-1395-1
ISBN 0-8230-1395-2
Printed in China

First printing 2003

14 / 15

This book is dedicated to the memory of my father,
Winsor Hays Watson Jr.,
with deep love, admiration, and gratitude.

ACKNOWLEDGMENTS

The support and love of my family, especially my husband, Baxter, daughter, Liz, mother, Jan, brother, Win, and my late father, have been invaluable. At Watson-Guptill, I am grateful to Joy Aquilino, senior acquisitions editor, for her vision; to editor Robbie Capp, book designer Areta Buk, and cover designer Sivan Earnest, for availing me of their many talents; and to Hector Campbell, the project's production manager. My thanks go to the staff of Silvermine School of Art, in New Canaan, Connecticut, especially to Anne Connell and Lynne Arovas. Debbie Beaudry, Janie Bronson, Kari Lønning, Annie Wood, and Al Roberts—friends with generous hearts and great "eyes"—gave me wonderful assistance. My gratitude goes to Putnam Imaging Lab in Danbury, Connecticut, in particular, to Josh Burkholder and Ed Simonovich. And a special, heartfelt thanks to the students at Silvermine who contributed directly to the creation of this book, as well as to the many others who allowed me to teach them and learn from them over the years.

ABOUT THE AUTHOR

CLAIRE WATSON GARCIA is an artist and instructor at the renowned Silvermine School of Art in New Canaan, Connecticut, where her "Absolute and Utter Beginner" courses and workshops have been popular for more than twenty years. She was educated at Smith College, University of California-Berkeley, and California College of Arts and Crafts. She lives in Ridgefield, Connecticut.

PHOTO BY KARI LØNNING

Contents

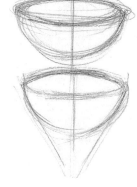

INTRODUCTION

Starting Out

"Every child is an artist. The problem is how to remain an artist once he grows up."

—PABLO PICASSO

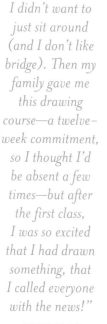

Do you want to learn to draw? You may have a feeling that you're meant to draw, that it could be fun, and might even become a significant part of your life. Your desire may even be a passionate one, as though you're being led to it by an invisible force. After all, our ancestors drew with rudimentary tools on the walls of caves, so there's historical precedent for our impulse to draw.

Maybe you've had a secret (or not so secret) wish for art in your life, and now you feel ready to act on it. You may be a parent who, stimulated by your child's love of art, wants some of that creative joy for yourself. Or perhaps you're a teacher who wants to help budding artists in the classroom, or a retiree looking for a rewarding way to spend free time. You may want to learn drawing fundamentals as a way to open the door to other art forms, like painting.

While there are many different paths to the art of drawing, everyone wants to learn this visual language in order to express what can't fully be expressed in words.

Drawing is a learnable skill, accessible to anyone who decides to activate his or her potential. You've already made a significant step in that direction simply by picking up a book on learning to draw. Being receptive to the possibility of drawing is the first important step toward acquiring the skill.

Now that you've taken that first step, the next step is to use a method designed to meet your needs as a beginner. *Drawing for the Absolute and Utter Beginner* is designed for people who want to explore their artistic side, but have no previous experience with art. You'll start at the very beginning, where you don't have to know anything at all about art or how to draw, and acquire technical skills and an understanding of how and when to use them in a logical, step-by-step manner.

Although I developed the studio course on which this book is based expressly for people with no artistic experience, it has also been useful to not-quite beginners, such as seasoned painters and graphic designers who may have missed a foundation in drawing. Photographers, familiar with composing images, may want to express with hand on paper what they've used a camera to record. Other not-quite beginners may have once been budding artists who began to develop their artistic potential but

"I learned that others often find something beautiful in what we self-judge as less than perfect. So it's more than learning the art of drawing. It's also about the art of self-acceptance."

—STUDENT ANITA ST. MARIE

8

were dissuaded from it or interrupted midstream. Perhaps an authority figure's unintentionally cruel remark derailed their artistic progress, or they were made to feel that it was wrong or impractical to pursue creative interests. For all those people, drawing remains much like a lost language, until finally, as adults, they are willing to explore their innate ability to draw as a means of expressing and sharing their feelings, thoughts, and impressions.

Drawing is to our experience of the visual world what handwriting is to our spoken language. If you can read this book and write your name, you can learn to draw.

Drawing is a universal, but underused, human capacity, well within reach of the so-called "average" person. But if this capacity is so natural to us, why is it that so few adults can draw? We were all artists in elementary school. Remember crayons and glue, scissors and paint? We felt comfortable using a visual means to express ourselves then. Yet, by adolescence, there are few artists left among us. Why is that the case?

Just as adult beginners aren't satisfied with drawing like a young child, many adolescents are equally embarrassed by their inability to record "acceptable" images on paper. This is not to say that representational art is preferable to childhood symbol art. It's simply that the expressive, symbolic art of the young child gives way to the older child's desire to portray a more literal view of the world. Basic drawing techniques can form the technical bridge between these two stages. But unless an effective program is available to teach those necessary new skills, there is no vehicle through which young artists can express their newly developed perspective on the world, and a natural artistic progression comes to a halt.

Among adolescent and adult beginners who do start the process of reviving their artistic life, many are focused on the talent quest. Much as they might want to develop their artistic potential, they fear they're destined to be a person with "no talent" who can "never learn to draw." But it's simply not the case that only a handful among us are equipped to pursue meaningful artistic expression. Drawing is a capacity that is developed, not something that springs fully formed from one's hands. The best way to learn how to draw is to forget about the talent quest and even any long-term drawing goal that you might have. Instead, this book asks you to focus only on the step-by-step instruction—a learning process designed to give you the understanding and skills needed to begin drawing with confidence.

"I was doing volunteer work at the Whitney Museum and thought it would be so wonderful if I myself could do something in art!"

—STUDENT BARBARA KOPS

"I doodled and wanted to go to art school. I had these pictures in my head that I wanted to get down on paper."

—STUDENT MICHELLE G. CAPPELLIERI

"I had always thought you can either draw or you can't draw. Now I've learned that if you practice drawing, you can get better at it. "

—STUDENT HELEN LOBRANO

9

How to Use This Book

By following the method outlined in this book, in less than a day's time, a beginner with no previous art experience can easily gain enough understanding of the basics to be able to draw recognizable objects and give them the illusion of dimension. You don't have to be a fast learner to achieve that goal. It's simply an indication of how close to the surface of your conscious awareness the drawing skill lies.

The chapter sequence is designed to provide a cumulative learning experience, with each chapter building on skills acquired in the previous one. The book maintains a linear sequence from Chapters 1 through 4, which contain drawing concepts that will give you a thorough understanding of the material presented in subsequent chapters. It's important to start at the very beginning, not only to get a clear idea and solid foundation, but also to acquire the confidence that comes with an understanding of the fundamentals. You'll

begin the drawing process with a totally "goof-proof" exercise, one that is instructive but also confidence building, so that you'll develop your skills from a fundamental point of success and understanding.

Along with the customary drawing techniques, I've included instruction in another all-important skill: the ability to evaluate your drawings constructively. This crucial tool allows you to accelerate your drawing progress and sidestep the tendency toward destructive evaluation. In effect, this book provides you with a private place to learn more about yourself and art, as well as a way to challenge such obstacles to learning as performance anxiety and harsh self-judgment.

THE BEGINNERS SPEAK

I've illustrated this book with drawings both by beginners and some not-quite beginners, all of whom have completed the same assignments. You'll be accompanied, as you learn, by their stories, tips, and encouragement. It's fascinating to see that even beginners have an innate preference for certain shapes, visual contrasts, and rhythms that come through in their drawings. The same thing will happen with you, for this personal style appears immediately, without conscious effort, and is such an integral part of each person's approach to drawing, that it doesn't change. You simply learn how to express it in the most complete and fulfilling way as your technical skills develop.

Approach drawing as a magical activity to do, to learn, and to see— profound, mysterious, and gratifying. Guided by the sequence of instruction and wise words from fellow beginners, you'll have an art adventure—full of challenges, yes, but discoveries and rewards as well.

"What pulled me into this drawing course was looking at young children and loving their freedom of expression and thinking, I want to do what they do! That freedom and then, the learning."
—STUDENT T. HAFFNER

Supplies

The following materials are the ones students have used with most success in my classes. Many of these items are available at most art-supply shops, but under "Miscellaneous," there are a few household items from the supermarket, and—very important—from a hardware store, a specific wire that you will need at the start of Chapter 1, so I urge you to shop for that first. Where certain brands of artists' materials are suggested, if you substitute others, keep in mind the specifications noted for that item. As you work your way through the book, you'll be reminded of which supplies are needed for specific exercises, as selected from the list below.

PAPERS
- *14"-×-17" drawing pad (Strathmore 400 series, 80-lb) for dry media and light washes*
- *6"-×-8" or 8"-×-10" drawing pad (same Strathmore series)*
- *14"-×-17" newsprint pad, medium or rough surface (not smooth)*
- *19"-×-25" pastel paper, 2 gray sheets (Canson Mi-Teintes)*
- *scrap paper (copier/computer/white craft)*

DRAWING MEDIA
- *2H, 2B, 6H, 6B drawing pencils*
- *2 black waterproof drawing pens (Uni-ball Vision micro and fine nibs)*
- *Conté crayons, 2 each, black and white, 2B*
- *vine charcoal sticks, medium or soft (package of 12)*

WET MEDIA
- *small tube black watercolor paint (any .27 tube)*
- *#6 "round" brush for acrylic or watercolor, with soft hairs that come to a point (Princeton Brush #4050)*

ERASERS AND BLENDERS
- *kneaded eraser*
- *Pink Pearl eraser*
- *2 writing-pencil erasers*
- *Q-Tips*

MISCELLANEOUS
- *24-gauge galvanized steel wire (small roll)*
- *fixative spray (Krylon workable for charcoal)*
- *paper towels, facial tissues*
- *water jar*
- *disposable palette: plastic or plastic-coated paper plate or freezer paper (Reynolds)*
- *tool box or ordinary shoe box to hold supplies*
- *artist's masking tape*

OPTIONAL
- *drawing board, 23" × 27" (extra support for drawing pads)*
- *portfolio (to store pads and finished work)*
- *2B charcoal pencil*
- *stump or tortillon (for blending charcoal and pastel)*
- *clip-on light*

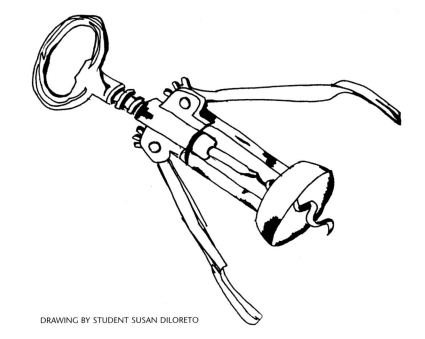

DRAWING BY STUDENT SUSAN DILORETO

CHAPTER 1

Seeing to Draw

*"What I put down in a moment of ardor,
I must then critically examine."*

—PETER ILYICH TCHAIKOVSKY

As enthusiastic as they are to begin drawing, beginners are often hesitant to put that first mark on paper. A student of mine described her feeling to me quite vividly: "My nerves were raw as I sat with virgin white paper and clutched pencil that first lesson. I felt that if I could avoid bringing the two in contact with each other, I could escape failure."

Nerves are a natural part of starting something new and exciting, and that's not all bad. Anxiety provides us with psychic rocket fuel, the adrenaline that pushes us to leap into new territory with quickened responses and heightened alertness. If you're feeling a bit jittery right now, take some scrap paper and simply scribble, mark, doodle, procrastinate, and "mess up the paper" until you have burned off some of that nervous energy.

*Avoid doing a verbal play-by-play while you draw.
Instead, try to empty your mind of words.
You'll find it easier to draw if you allow time for
nonverbal, visual processing.*

When you're fixated on the result and wondering if you have enough "talent" to draw, you can't pay attention to acquiring drawing skills; the talent search diverts you from the pleasure of drawing. The greatest enjoyment lies in the artistic journey rather than in the final destination.

In order to benefit emotionally as well as technically—and they work together—place your focus on each of the exercises as you get to them. Follow the mountain-climber's caveat: Don't look back or too far ahead; look for the useful footholds. Every mark you put on paper serves your purpose, either by showing you what you did right or what needs to be strengthened.

SUPPLIES FOR
THIS CHAPTER
2B pencil
black drawing pen
24-gauge wire
14"-×-17" drawing pad
scrap paper

*"When we drew the
wire, I felt good.
I felt like the wire
had character and
I had captured that
in my drawing.
I was surprised by
that and thought,
Maybe this will
work for me!"*

—STUDENT RITA WALKER
COPPING

OPPOSITE:
The greatest
enjoyment lies in
the artistic journey
rather than the
final destination.

Recording Edges: Contour Drawing

Try out an adventurous "let's see what happens" attitude in approaching the contour exercises that lie ahead. Here, at the very beginning, you aren't expected to know anything and you can't fail. There's no competition involved. You're learning to draw, a specific, accessible skill, not searching for talent. Your final drawing is simply a record of your learning process.

EXERCISE: WIRE DRAWING
Read these directions through once completely, before you begin to draw. After that, don't read and draw at the same time; to remind yourself of the exercise sequence, just refer to the following **Summary of Essentials:**

- *Use pencil for drawing #1.*
- *Use pen for drawings #2 and #3.*
- *Slow down and observe carefully.*
- *Use one, slowly executed, continuous dark line.*
- *Record every twist and turn in the wire.*
- *Change the shape of your wire after each drawing.*

1 Place your open pad in front of you. Remove a piece of drawing paper and put it on the table next to your pad (to the left for righties, to the right for lefties).
2 With scissors, cut a 15" piece of wire from the roll and bend it into a shape that appeals to you, leaving the ends loose. If you've made something that sticks way up, flatten it down a little.
3 Put your wire on the loose paper next to your pad to see your wire more clearly. Move the wire around until you find a view that you can settle on. You're going to draw on the pad. Tilt the pad if it feels more comfortable that way.
4 Look at your wire. You don't have to memorize the shape, just begin the process of observation, taking in bends and bumps from one end to the other.

5 Hold your pencil naturally, as you would when writing. Put your pencil point on the paper at a spot that will correspond to one end of your wire. Once your pencil point touches the paper, don't lift it until you've recorded the entire wire, from end to end.
6 Slowly, very slowly, begin to record what you see—every change, every bend in the wire, with one dark, continuous line. If you're a speed demon who charges through intersections you'll have a challenge here. The slower you go, the more you'll benefit.
7 Look back and forth between pencil and wire as you work, keeping your pencil on the paper at all times, without lifting it. Proceed v-e-r-r-y slowly. You are not going to erase, so make your marks show. Press down and watch a nice dark line emerge from your pencil point. Record the wire until you reach the end.
8 Do at least two more drawings—but use your black pen this time. Maintain a slow pace. Eraser is forbidden—so be bold!

Reminder: Now that you've read the exercise instructions, begin to draw. So you can draw without reading, refer to the **Summary of Essentials** (left).

RE-VIEW YOUR WIRE DRAWING
One myth about artists is that creativity flows from their fingertips. However, art flows principally from the artist's mind, and numerous techniques are used to improve the work. One of the most fundamental tricks of the trade is simply stepping back to evaluate work, and then developing a strategy for further action. Artwork is routinely re-viewed— literally, viewed again and again—in every creative field; any experienced artist will confirm that time-honored strategy. So, put on an artist's beret, if it gets you more in the mood, and let's re-view.

GAINING PERSPECTIVE ON YOUR DRAWING

Stand up and look down at your drawings. Do they look somewhat different from that distance and perspective? Did you:

- *Slow down (no speed demons here) and observe carefully?*
- *Record what you saw as specifically (no generalities) as you could?*
- *Make continuous, dark, firm imprints (no sketchy, light, or broken lines) with your pencil and pen?*

Did you fulfill any of the above objectives? If you did, then fulfill one more: Admit it if you did *anything* right. Out loud is good! That last objective is the single most important one.

Over the years, the wire-drawing exercise has shown me that each person, given a choice of thousands of possibilities, will tend to replicate certain shapes, with variations. While I can't tell you what the shapes mean, they do indicate personal aesthetic preferences, unique to each of us, and as individual as our thumbprint. How do you like *your* own lines? If they are continuous and firm, they will be strong, definite, confident-looking, rhythmic—and handsome.

Contour drawing has its own way of communicating, comparable to a dialect. As you progress through these pages, you'll see that different qualities are conveyed by different types of line, similar to nuances in speaking. If you hear muffled, hesitant speech, the speaker may appear confused or shy, reluctant to communicate. With drawing, pen lines may seem more confident than pencil lines because they show up more boldly. If they are relatively fluid and unbroken, they're like confident speakers—those who express themselves fluently, self-assuredly.

When you begin to evaluate your work constructively, you're going to be less afraid of mistakes. Once you learn more about technique and can identify what doesn't work, you can take an active part in improving your drawing, rather than being a passive onlooker when it comes to fixing problems.

If you didn't fulfill the objective of the above exercise but you understand why, wait a day and try again. Lots of us find it hard to slow down the first time. Beginners often associate a fast, sketchy approach with the ability to draw well, and they equate slowness with incompetence. Sketches improve after we learn to slow down and observe with care and precision. When you allow yourself time to look, you give yourself time to learn.

Consider taking a break then starting again, once you've digested this much. A break is an art sorbet; it refreshes you between drawing courses.

Once you've started to observe closely, record carefully, and appreciate the quality of line that emerges from contour drawing, you're ready to move to the next step. But be sure to keep your wire drawings and all your drawings from now on. We'll use them for an important exercise at the very end.

Looking at these wire drawings of fellow beginners, do you see differences among them—a repetition of certain shapes by each individual— long lines, curled ones, loops, angles? Often there is a consistency of shapes on a page that looks something like handwriting. Do you see that on your page?

STUDENT DRAWINGS, FROM LEFT, BY BARBARA KOPS, ANNE BALLANTYNE, SANDY FITZMAURICE.

Recording Shapes Upside Down

No, you don't have to stand on your head to do the next exercise! Copy the image on this page, then later, the one on page 18, just as they are, upside down; if you turn them right side up, it will put you at a disadvantage. These images are already exaggerated and somewhat goofy, so don't be concerned if you make them look strange or out of proportion. They already are. In fact, you'll probably improve them.

Avoid identifying parts of the image in words. Just imagine what you see as made of wire. Think *wire* if it keeps your mind away from other words. Don't be concerned if what you produce is larger or smaller than the original. Any scale will do. If you happen to run off the page, it means your concentration is focused on line, which is fine. Forget about proportion, because you don't have the tools to deal with that yet. Since the original drawing is already out of proportion, yours will be too. Thinner, fatter, longer, smaller, or missing some line is fine.

Sustain your firm, slow line. Stay with "slow and steady"; it wins the race for this exercise. You'll build up necessary understanding. Take time to develop a strategy before you begin. You need to lift your pen with this exercise, but only when you want to.

EXERCISE: UPSIDE-DOWN DRAWING
Read the following material through completely before you start to draw the image on this page. Reread the exercise if you need to before copying the image on page 18. Continue working with your pen to help you avoid pale and hesitant lines. To avoid reading while drawing, refer to this **Summary of Essentials:**

* *Maintain your slow pace.*
* *Observe carefully.*
* *Record every change you see in the drawings provided.*
* *Use as many long lines as you need.*
* *Lift your pen when it makes sense to do so.*

1 Begin with a long line that starts at the top of the page, and follow it until you reach the end of that line. If you find intersecting lines or ones that

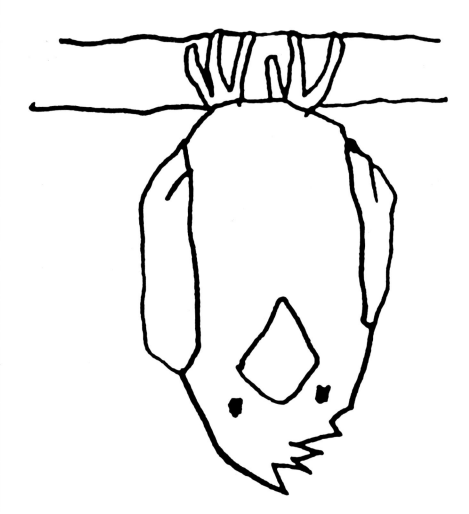

Keep your paper upside down until you finish drawing. If you turn it around before then, you'll defeat the purpose of this exercise. Upside-down drawing is a technique that will help reinforce your growing ability to see and report on shapes and edges.

move toward the interior of the image, put those in next.

2 Lift your pencil from the paper when your line comes to an end. Sometimes you'll backtrack over the line a bit. That's fine. Just don't reiterate a line because you're wondering if you did it right.

3 Draw in clusters, following a major line, then taking care of smaller lines that branch out from it. Then return to the major line. There is no one best way to approach this. Simply follow a sequence that makes sense to you in order to replicate the image. However, it is usually more difficult to outline the entire image first, then try to fill it in, or to start up one side and the other simultaneously, then try to make them meet.

4 False starts and dead ends aren't serious mistakes. Regard them as signposts of momentum. No mistakes equals nothing ventured—and you know what that means! So if you get lost or make the wrong line, just simply *stop*. Figure out where you have to go, and begin a fresh line where it seems logical. The quality of your line—specific and dark—matters more than perfect placement.

5 Your drawing is an ongoing process of depicting on a flat surface what you understand at that moment about what you see, then learning again from what you see in your drawing. Without so-called mistakes, you can't learn how to draw.

6 When you finish recording everything, turn the page around and compare it with the original—both right side up. If you have anything that looks like the original image, congratulate yourself! Remember, you're looking for ballpark likeness, not a photocopy.

Reminder: Now that you've read the exercise instructions, begin to draw. So you can draw without reading, refer to the **Summary of Essentials** (page 16).

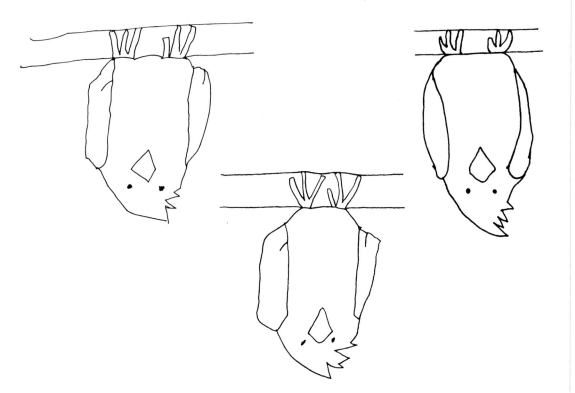

A crucial objective of upside-down drawing is developing the ability to see what works, a strategy that is clearly working where these beginners' results are concerned. STUDENT DRAWINGS, FROM LEFT, BY BARBARA KOPS, AMY MILLER, PAMELA M. HEBERTON

CONSTRUCTIVE EVALUATION

Place your drawings on or against a wall when you're finished, rather than simply looking down at them. You need some distance to evaluate your work constructively. Does the page have a new impact at a distance? Were you able to:

- *Maintain a slow pace and observe carefully?*
- *Retain some continuous lines?*
- *Reproduce a comparable image?*

If you met those objectives, congratulate yourself! The most important aim here is to find your success and claim it. Not perfection, but some aspect, no matter how small, that you did right. You can't climb the mountain unless you find small, secure footholds.

"When I describe my drawing experience, I hope it encourages other beginners. I found out that I could do it, and I saw everyone around me doing it. Also, that everyone does it differently, and what begins to come out is a sort of inner truth for each individual, some sort of life theme or life mood."
—STUDENT JULIA GARDINER

Check in on your fellow beginners to see how they did. What you see is simply what happens time after time in class. Everyone does it. Namely, they are able to replicate the original images, more or less accurately. And while precision in itself is a positive, a high degree of accuracy may not be what makes a drawing wonderful. It can be spacing between objects, unexpected scale, degree of animation and interaction—surprising aspects that weren't consciously created.

STUDENT DRAWINGS, FROM LEFT, BY BARBARA KOPS, PAMELA M. HEBERTON, AMY MILLER

Why does this approach work? Drawing is a visual language. It describes the look of an object in line, shape, and value, rather than describing it in words. Upside-down drawing forces us to see shapes and lines in order to make sense of the image.

When you did the exercises in this chapter and focused wordlessly on those interlocking puzzle pieces of line and shape, duplicating the pattern you saw, you drew the likeness before you without quite thinking about it. You were looking at the world the way an artist does, focusing on the parts that make up the visual whole. Rather than learning how to draw "trees," a generic verbal category, artists pay attention to the contours, shadows, and shapes of the particular form they want to draw—tree, face, flower, dish—in order to capture the special quality of their visual experience.

PLAYER AND COACH

It's not necessary or helpful to your drawing process to eliminate words or stay "in the moment" at all times. You can scan the results of your drawing and come to some conclusions to identify what works and what you want to improve next time. Then you can draw again with a more precise idea of what needs to be done. You alternate your capacities to develop your ability to draw.

The alternating roles you're using are similar to the ideal relationship between player and coach. The player (you) takes an active, physical role (drawing), based on an understanding of the rules and skills required in the game. The coach (also you) then provides constructive verbal evaluation of play from the sidelines (constructive review), but not while the player is playing. The mutual goal of this relationship is to improve performance.

Player and coach fulfill distinct, complementary, but also potentially conflicting, roles. For example, a player can't benefit from advice if the coach shouts comments from the bleachers while the player's game is going smoothly. Nor should a player run all over the court while the coach tries to discuss the previous match and expect to learn anything. Alternating these roles is necessary and effective for them and, by extension, for you. Otherwise, chaos rules.

All of us have experiences that are fluid, automatic, based on a clear understanding of what's going on. Typing, cooking, walking, if familiar, don't require evaluation, words, or self-critique. When tasks in everyday life are fluid and seem automatic, you are in that player mode. When an impasse occurs or an active episode is finished, the coach steps in to offer advice and solve problems. The presence of your coach is recognized when evaluation and using words begins.

This is a skill-set we use everyday as human beings. We drive the car around happily, until it starts clunking and fuming—then we take it in for repair, and drive it again once it's fixed. Giving yourself the opportunity for wordless activity (player), when applied to art, is simply a new application of a very familiar skill. You just have to hold the door open into that wordless capacity long enough (without needless or ineffectual interruption) to have it continue to emerge.

If you expect your art to develop without use of your critical skill (coach), you'll limit yourself. Why not apply a powerful capacity at your disposal to accelerate your development? You simply need to learn how to apply it constructively, so you can evaluate your work. As we proceed, you'll learn more about how to apply this skill-set harmoniously, along with other techniques.

"I found it very compelling, but also relaxing. You'd work on something and then look up, and two hours would have floated by."
—STUDENT BOB PINGARRON

Homework

Once you've finished the primary upside-down exercises on the previous pages, try other images, using the same technique. For starters, work with the drawing below. Then, compare your upside-down results with those of your fellow beginners shown here.

For this image, as with the earlier upside-down exercises, begin with a long line at the top of your page. Maintain a slow pace, observe carefully, record every change you see.

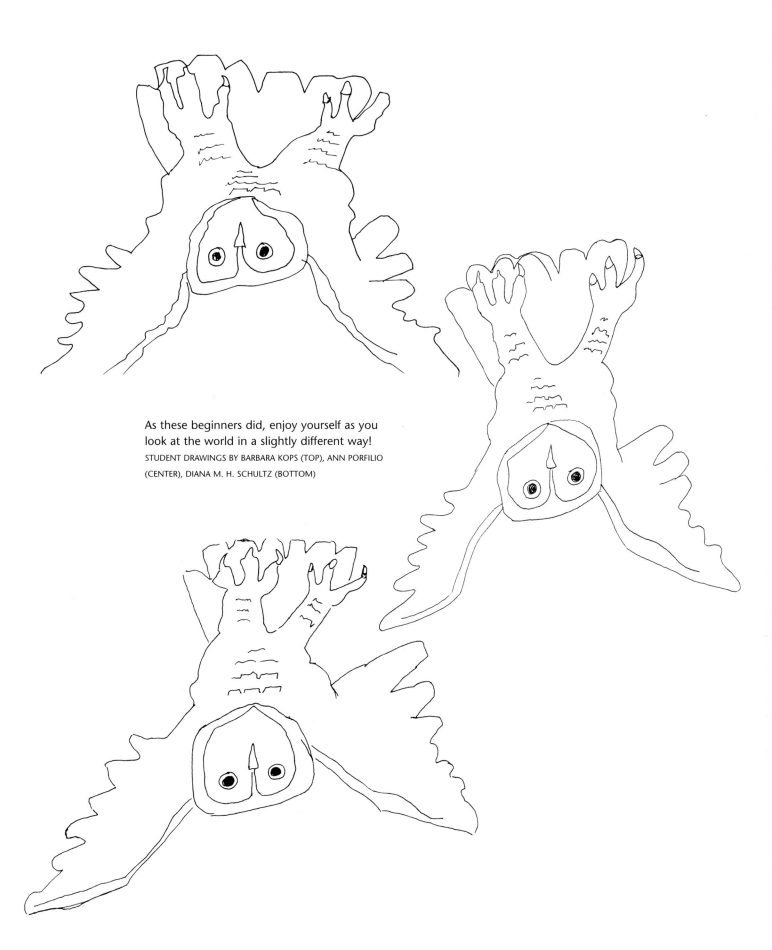

As these beginners did, enjoy yourself as you look at the world in a slightly different way!
STUDENT DRAWINGS BY BARBARA KOPS (TOP), ANN PORFILIO (CENTER), DIANA M. H. SCHULTZ (BOTTOM)

CHAPTER 2

Turning Edges into Objects

*"In a way, nobody sees a flower really. It is so small,
we haven't time—like to have a friend takes time."*

—GEORGIA O'KEEFFE

Now that you can replicate shapes and edges with some success, let's apply that skill to drawing three-dimensional objects. Read through the material in this section completely, including "Problem Solvers" (page 26), before starting to draw.

To find subject matter, collect objects from around your home. Detailed, segmented, articulated tools and equipment from the kitchen, garage, and hobbies are great choices. Leaves, sliced fruit, flowers, onions, and slotted spoons all work well. Radishes with leaves and scallions with roots are highly recommended. Use the illustrations in this section as a guide.

*A glance of the eye doesn't move along a shape,
observing details; it lands on one spot. A long
observation collects lots of information for you—
quite literally—to draw from.*

Choose objects that mean something to you. For instance, if you love to work with plants and flowers, garden tools may cause you to connect with your subject matter more energetically. However, you need to feel an interest in the shapes you see, not just in the activity associated with the tools you choose.

Stay away from plain, smooth objects or anything that's so complicated that you may be asking for a bad time. Lamps, crystal, decoy ducks, and rounded sculptures seem to be frequent bad choices for beginners. Choosing the best subjects can take some time. Treat it as a treasure hunt!

Separate your treasures into three categories: objects that are relatively flat (brushes, spatulas); those with overlapping parts (scissors, eyeglasses); and those with more spatial depth (cookie cutters). The last group is the most challenging to draw.

Put one chosen object on white paper so you can see its edges more clearly. Arrange it in a way that appeals to you. We've taken to calling this your "beloved" in my class, because the attraction should be strong.

SUPPLIES FOR
THIS CHAPTER

black drawing pen
14"-×-17" drawing pad
scrap paper

*"Don't draw for the
end product. Enjoy
the process. I'd
have so much fun,
I'd forget to worry
about the finished
product, and it
worked out much
better that way."*

—STUDENT SHERRY
ARTEMENKO

OPPOSITE:

DRAWING BY STUDENT

PATRICIA P. SPOOR

Look Before You Leap

"I love that coffeepot. It's from my mother. The stories it could tell! I know the drawing is out of proportion, but part of me loves it because of that. And I love the line and shape of it." —STUDENT T. HAFFNER

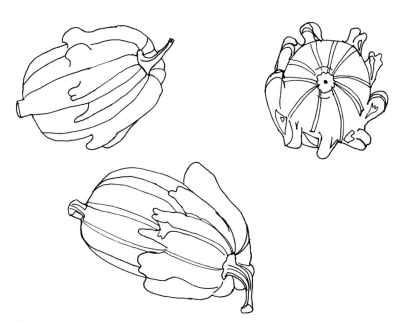

"When we discuss the 'beloved' object in class, for me, that object is something that attracts me. Then I enjoy developing a drawing of it—that special enjoyment of the creative process." —STUDENT PAMELA M. HEBERTON

To get the best results when applying your contour-drawing technique to three-dimensional objects, look carefully before drawing, and sustain long lines wherever possible. Digest the edge in front of you; don't just glance and go. Give your eyes time to move along the edge of the object you're going to draw, until you truly comprehend it. Project the shape of that line from start to finish on your paper so you get a brief feel for starting point and destination. When you draw, you can follow the pattern of the line you've projected.

SLOW, DELIBERATE APPROACH

Approach your chosen object as you did in Chapter 1, maintaining your contour-drawing technique. Don't worry about the predictable wiggles and lack of a full three-dimensional look. And before you begin any exercises in this chapter, to avoid reading while drawing, refer to the following **Summary of Essentials:**

- *Continue to draw slowly.*
- *Use long, continuous, dark lines.*
- *Sustain lines as long as it makes sense to do so.*
- *Break lines when necessary.*
- *Record contours of the objects you observe.*

Look for a long horizontal or diagonal line at the top of your object as a starting place. Pick a line you think you can do and/or want to try. Stay with slow pressure; don't lift your hand until it's logical to do so. Think of every edge as "wire," nothing tentative. Any edge that can be turned into line, including the sharp edge of a highlight, do so. Solid, unequivocal black can be used for black areas.

"I chose this sieve because it reminded me of one my parents have—including the peeling handle, which I did first and worked up from there to the metal rim around the mesh. I drew all the wires in one direction first, to capture the dents in the mesh, then connected the crosswires coming from the opposite direction." —STUDENT RITA WALKER COPPING

Pay attention to the edges of objects. If a machine-made tool has a top surface and an identifiable side surface, be sure to draw both, even if it's a set of very narrow parallel lines (as along the edge of a slotted spoon). This, and changes in line direction accurately reported, will give you more depth than you anticipated. DRAWING BY STUDENT SANDY FITZMAURICE

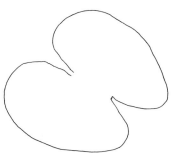

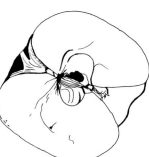

Helen's effective use of solid black areas adds a dynamic element to the overall pattern and increases the dramatic impact of her drawing. DRAWING BY STUDENT HELEN LOBRANO

"I do a lot of work outside, so I find those tools more interesting than kitchen implements, for example. There's something less domesticated about the clippers and the bolt cutter—something I'd call a bit vicious. But at the same time, I am very fond of them, and they're fun to draw. Now, when I use them, I see them differently, almost like living things—like fish that have evolved with extreme oddities. I like following their shapes, their construction, putting pieces together."

—STUDENT JULIA GARDINER

Problem Solvers

To translate a three-dimensional object into a two-dimensional drawing, develop a strategy that gives you a mental/visual run-through of how you'll approach the challenge. With a gesture of your hand over the surface of your paper, you can replicate the general space your drawing will occupy, to get a preliminary feel for its general shape and dimensions. Notice how aspects of the shape connect. Look over the object, taking in its shape, deciding where you'll start and generally where you'll go. To enter the drawing, pick a long line you can follow. Take small pauses throughout as you decide your next moves.

"One of the things I learned was to just keep going. It was frustrating because I'm doing a leaf outline, and not seeing it yet. I would say to myself, Just forget about it! Just wait until the end. You can always do another one, or start over again."

—STUDENT TRACEY M. ROBINSON

GETTING LOST
Line quality is highly significant in contour drawing. If you goof and get lost, don't give up, and don't point out your goof by crossing out. The bold confidence of the line is broken more by crossouts than by an inaccurate line. Once you're finished, you'll be surprised how little a few mismarks will matter—what is seen at viewing distance is different from what you see at "doing distance." Instead of calling attention to an inconsequential slip by crossing it out, your strategy is to calmly pick up at the right place and keep going. If you are nervous about continuing, remind yourself that it's only a drawing. You can always do another!

TEDIOUS RELATIONSHIPS
Don't feel compelled to draw the same object until you "get it right." This should be an ideal relationship, so just let it go if it wasn't your true beloved. Substitute an object that you like better, and start over with new energy. You'll find that some objects will stimulate you to work in a more focused way.

BENDS
Your drawings of machine-made objects won't look like they came straight out of a catalogue. They'll look slightly animated, perhaps distorted. At this point, just concentrate on seeing, recording, and maintaining the contour line. You can add more accuracy in the next chapter.

DIFFICULT PARTS
If you see something you know will give you trouble, practice that portion on scrap paper until you feel you've learned the shapes a bit. Spiral shapes, like corkscrews, are prime candidates.

"Everything seems difficult at first. That feeling vanishes as I just draw."

—STUDENT JULIA GARDINER

PERSPECTIVE
Beginners often use the word "perspective" to indicate their concern with giving dimension to objects. But perspective is not an issue at this point, since you won't get much spatial depth from contour drawing anyway, although you might get more than you expect.

NEGATIVE SPACE
When you draw a slotted spoon, for example, the little space shapes created by the cutout slots are called negative spaces.

Check out the illustrations on these pages to see how often it's the shape of what's *not* there—the negative space—surrounded by what is there, that adds, or even attracts, the most interest.

OVERLAPS

Objects with overlapping parts seem to give beginners amazing powers of X-ray vision. Superman may indeed see traffic right through a highway overpass as he flies by, but we need to draw *only* what we are able to see, not what we know is there. We know one blade of a scissors exists under the other, but we see only part of that blade—and that's the part to draw.

SO-CALLED MISTAKES

If you don't get it just right, you can learn from that glitch, storing up the sight and feel manually of what you'll avoid next time. Every line teaches you something about how to draw. Keep in mind that drawings rarely conform to the artist's vision. Artwork has a secret life of its own. You're in for constant surprises when drawing. You may not be able to recognize what is in your drawing at first, simply because it isn't ever quite what you anticipated.

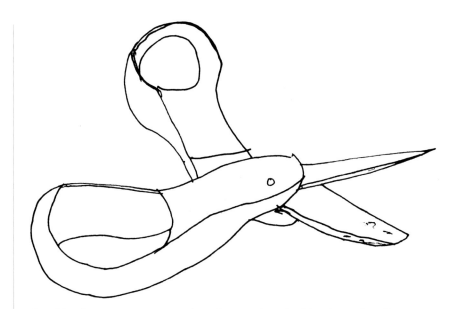

An object's empty spaces—such as the openings in this scissors handle—are negative spaces. If you can draw the shape of a negative space, you can draw the positive one better, since they share common edges. Shapes of negative spaces also exist between objects, although they are often not as precise. The space between objects becomes charged the closer they are to one another. Edges of the paper, untouched by the pen, are remote and devoid of drama by comparison. DRAWING BY STUDENT BARBARA KOPS

When dealing with overlapping parts of an object, as in these keys, preview how you'll approach the drawing before you touch pen to paper. Draw the "over"—the "on top" part—first. Then draw the "under" part around it, leaving out the area that can't be seen. Note where the line has to stop to avoid the X-ray pitfall. DRAWING BY STUDENT AL ROBERTS

Re-Viewing Your 3D Drawings

BREAK BEFORE YOU BREAK

Take breaks—not in the middle of doing a small drawing, but afterward, and between drawings. Break as often as you need to recharge your energy. Remember, quality, not quantity, is the point.

When you've completed two or three objects, put your page of drawings up on a wall and study them. Did you:

- *Maintain the contour-drawing technique, going slowly, using pressure?*
- *Draw a recognizable object?*
- *Draw what you saw, not what you knew was there?*

If you had some success with the above objectives, even if limited, give yourself credit. You're headed in the right direction. Check in on your fellow beginners to see how they did. Pick out work you like and see if you can identify why you like it. Are there objects you enjoy looking at, not only because they are accurate or recognizable, but simply because you enjoy their shapes and movement?

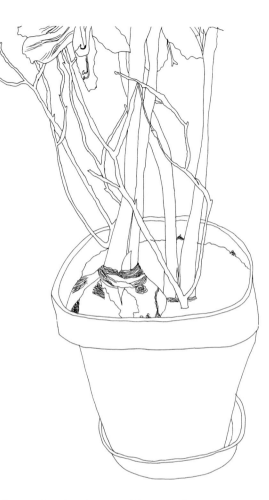

When a drawing has repetitive angular shapes, as in this plant, the eye follows those reference points, stimulated by the rhythm of the drawing, which seems faster and more animated. Rounder shapes literally have fewer reference "points," and therefore give a more flowing, peaceful impression. Don't be concerned if an exercise drawing runs off the page, such as the leaves at the top of this plant. As mentioned earlier, it simply means that the artist's concentration is focused on line, just as it should be. DRAWING BY STUDENT JOAN SIMONELLI

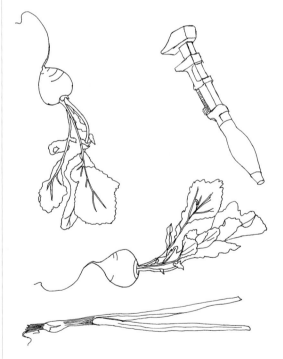

Spontaneous placement of objects on the page creates movement and pattern that becomes more visible from a distance. Negative spaces created between the objects (which are the positive spaces) take on greater significance. DRAWING BY STUDENT PAMELA M. HEBERTON

Locating What's Good

In the drawing course I teach, during the first class, which covers the material you're working on now, I ask students to find and share something they like about a fellow beginner's work. My students always respond with enthusiasm. But when I ask them to share aloud what's good about their own artwork, they find it far more difficult to do so. Initially, most students only point to what they don't like about their work. They argue that they can't see anything good—a different argument from saying there isn't anything good to see. And inevitably, one beginner will admire the very qualities in the drawing of another student who feels unsure or negative about that same artwork.

Locating what's good is a practical skill. It means knowing what to look for and how to identify it in words. Saying it aloud isn't necessary when looking at one's own work; however, it's not a bad idea. Putting perceptions into words can give you more clarity when evaluating work.

Students frequently review their first drawings for evidence as to whether they deserve to be artists or not. Harsh self-assessment presents the greatest obstacle by far to the development of artistic potential. Sometimes I feel that beginners are hard on themselves as protection. If they preempt others by saying something harsh about their own work, they haven't left themselves open to hearing the imagined critical remark from someone else.

To help banish such unproductive, self-limiting criticism, we're going to expand the method of constructive evaluation we have used thus far. The following may look a bit like the kindergarten bulletin board, but remember, we were all artists back then.

- *Treat your artistic side politely, as you would a friend. Don't crush this new relationship with rudeness and cruelty. Would you want to keep company with someone who insults you?*
- *Limit any criticism to three specific points that need your attention.*
- *Find some small thing that you did right. This is a practical measure, not sentiment. It gives you a model to follow.*
- *Develop techniques. Once you know how to identify what works, what doesn't, and how to fix problems, you will fear mistakes less and move ahead more rapidly.*
- *Make improvement your focus, not criticism.*

Careful observation of contour and shape—from creases in leather to the movement of textured laces—give this boot the specific presence and character of a portrait. DRAWING BY STUDENT DEBORAH L. JANTZ-SELL

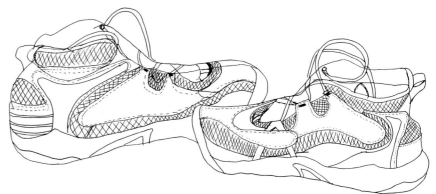

Typical of this student's work, the objects she chooses to draw show her underlying attraction for shapes that have interwoven pathways, as in this pair of running shoes. DRAWING BY STUDENT KATHY EPSTEIN

"I always take breaks now, because I see with new eyes when I come back to my work. They can be short breaks or longer."
—STUDENT KIM NIGHTINGALE

Claiming Your Success

Being positive about one's accomplishment, no matter how small, is more challenging than identifying what's wrong. Many beginners can easily find what's not working, but rarely what's good. Perhaps they think it seems immodest to claim a success, that it runs counter to what society teaches us is acceptable. But skillful students are able to identify the right path, the sturdy footholds in their work, so they know how to proceed. Take your lead from them. Finding what works, no matter how small, needs to be part of your method because:

- *It provides the incentive to fix what isn't working. After all, why develop the ability to improve anything if there's nothing worth fixing?*
- *It gives you an example to follow, so you can mimic the specific qualities of line that are successful in your work.*
- *You need it to maintain your drawing progress because ultimately, you're the one who is in charge of your work.*

Identifying what works develops your powers of observation as well as nourishing your self-confidence. This constructive approach will help you to see the larger picture in the drawing process. It will put into perspective those imperfect results that are bound to occur as you learn skills you've never had before.

Think of walking, of learning your native language, all much more complex than this process will be. Your approach to drawing will not be all accepting and unconditional. It will be a balance between recognizing what works and what doesn't, and using your growing skill repertoire from which to choose the tools needed to fix what needs fixing. By exercising your capacity for constructive evaluation, you will learn how to be both player and coach effectively.

This doesn't mean negative comments have no place in the process. Get it out there! With every classroom of beginners, I hear a chorus of frustrated grumbles and complaints, so you are not alone or odd if you do the same. By all means, moan and groan if any particular level of frustration gets to you. However, practicing the constructive approach will help you to "get back on the horse" and keep moving ahead. Complaining and learning to be a constructive critic are both integral parts of learning to draw.

YOUR DRAWING EXPERIENCE NOW

You may have had the experience of locking into a particular object, committing intense energy and interest to exploring the shape and line you saw. You may have felt unaware of time passing. This type of experience, almost like being mesmerized by what you see, usually yields strong and interesting work.

The objects you've drawn may be distorted or slightly out of proportion as compared with the originals. But it's just that quality that gives them character—that may actually turn inanimate objects into animated characters. If there is more than one image on a page in your drawing pad, those characters may seem to be in an emotionally charged relationship. What would they say if they could speak to one another? How would someone else interpret that page? If you aren't too shy, show it to a relative or friend and ask what those characters suggest to them.

Artists create relationships between inanimate objects—fruit, flowers, teacups, wine glasses—where no real connection exists. Artists project their own human vitality into landscape and still life, as well as into pure abstract shapes. You may see evidence of this creative vitality in the animation of your own objects. The "distortion" isn't a mistake. It's a gift.

In a classroom full of beginners or artists at any level, each person will draw the same objects differently, though recognizably. By now, you may see some evidence of your own innate aesthetic, that unique and automatic preference for a certain scale, shape, rhythm—something very central to your individuality. It's already there. You just need to learn how to let it show in a more fully realized manner.

When you have as your goal the careful inspection of shapes and edges that make up specific items, everyday objects like these can take on heightened visual appeal. STUDENT DRAWINGS, FROM TOP, BY TRACEY M. ROBINSON, JANE WOLANSKY, KATHY EPSTEIN

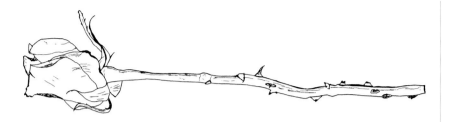

You've begun to understand that if you want to learn how to represent a recognizable image, the way to do it is to forget about the generic concept of the object and concentrate instead on the visual component parts that make up its overall image. During periods of active drawing, you have learned to leave behind the words you used effectively in the past to define your perception of an object—as in, "That's a beautiful flower"—and give precedence to observing and recording the particular patterns of the specific flower that attracts you.

You've begun a new visual orientation, comparable to slipping new software into a perfectly capable computer. Your eye and mind are accustomed to looking at the world for the purpose of recognizing "flower." Now they need time to adjust to your new goal: the careful inspection of the shapes and edges that make up a specific flower, so that you can draw it with greater confidence and individuality.

"I love roses, their scent, their shape and color—how straight lines could blend into sharp, jagged curves so fluidly. At first, I was fearful to just let the pen go. Somehow as each line progressed, I felt the rose taking shape. I liked what I saw, even though it wasn't an exact duplicate. Building on each petal gave me a sense of excitement to see the finished product, and I didn't mind if it took hours." —STUDENT KRISTEN NIMR

A dramatic encounter between dinosaurlike tools and a reticent radish wasn't the conscious intent of this artist, but the natural result of the energy transferred to inanimate objects in the drawing process. DRAWINGS BY STUDENT ANN PORFILIO

Homework

The instinct that got you to open this book and start drawing can continue to play a crucial part in the success of your endeavor. I encourage you to keep your go-ahead spirit going. You can do as much or as little as is comfortable. Think of this process as learning something about drawing, rather than feeling you have to learn everything about drawing all at once.

You can now represent anything you see in contour line, although not yet as realistically, accurately, or convincingly as you would wish. You've seen and experienced that line has inherent qualities aside from its utility in representing recognizable objects. We'll make use of the sketched line next, both to add accuracy techniques, and for just plain fun.

Most important is to do at least two more contour drawings of three-dimensional objects, maintaining the contour-drawing technique. Use your pen; it will keep you from equivocating.

"Something clicked inside my mind and I was able to see things differently. Instead of looking at what I was drawing as a whole thing, I looked at its parts."

—STUDENT TRACEY M. ROBINSON

"When I first walked into drawing class, I was seventy years old. I had never drawn anything in my life. And I was sure I couldn't, but I had always wanted to. I started drawing at the top of the handle and worked my way down. I drew the bristles last, starting on the left-hand side. It was at that point that the pen seemed to take off on its own, and I was amazed and thrilled at the result! —STUDENT SALLY MONAHAN

DRAWING BY STUDENT AL ROBERTS

CHAPTER 3

Adding Accuracy

*"All that is required is to release control.
Some part of ourselves will bring us into unison."*

—OSKAR KOKOSCHKA

What does the word *sketch* bring to mind? "Spontaneous" and "a quick impression" are the responses I hear most often. When you sketch, you draw in a direct, simple way to convey an impression. Many beginners come to my class or workshop specifically to learn how to sketch. The informal look of a sketch suggests that it's the most accessible kind of drawing.

So why don't I begin my classes with sketching? My experience has shown that beginners need to reorient their way of looking at things first. In everyday life, we use our sight to identify things—that's my house, my car, my big toe—not to analyze them for the purpose of drawing. Looking at things with the intention of drawing them makes a big difference. It requires focused looking, slowing down enough to observe the world first, before drawing.

You draw with your mind and eyes first. Drawing with your eyes while you go about your day can make mundane tasks much more interesting!

Sketching calls on our ability to look before we take that leap. That devotional time you spent contour drawing—which entailed slowing down and taking a good look—is the essential basis for all your drawing.

We're going to use the casual, loose, sketched line next. Paradoxically, sketching, which can look imprecise and even sloppy at times, will be your best friend now that it's time to add more accuracy to your drawing. You're going to use pencil again in this chapter because it best suits the fluidity and portability needed for a sketching technique.

We often hear this question posed about art and artists: "How do they do that?" Accuracy techniques play a large part in how it's done. Now it's time to explore and apply those techniques to your own drawing. The working routine you set for yourself, in terms of when and where you draw, also plays a major role, so let's start there.

SUPPLIES FOR THIS CHAPTER

2B pencil
Pink Pearl eraser
14"-x-17" rough newsprint pad
14"-x-17" drawing pad
6"-x-8" or 8"-x-10" drawing pad

"My place used to be so neat until I started doing art. Now there are piles of stuff everywhere!"

—STUDENT PAT PIZZO

OPPOSITE:
DRAWING BY STUDENT
DEBORAH L. JANTZ-SELL

A Time and Place to Draw

You'll need to set aside blocks of time to draw—solitary time, unless your focus is very strong, even in the face of noise and activity around you. Life easily fills in any extra pockets of time you have, so your only solution is to dedicate time to your drawing. On a calendar, designate a fixed time when you can draw, and pencil it in. Make a date with yourself. Just like going to the gym to get exercise for your body, you need to go to a place on a regular basis to exercise and develop your artistic capacity. Carve that time and place out for yourself.

"I like to draw at night, but my husband is always coming down and saying, It's after midnight and you should be in bed!"

—STUDENT RITA WALKER COPPING

Or do you already have a place to work? Since the practice of art is new to you, it's likely you've borrowed space in the kitchen or are sitting in the basement. You're not expected to build a studio yet—but to ensure that your family respects your space, it's a good idea to let them know what you're up to, especially if your model for a still life is something they might want to eat!

"I smashed our banister carrying my work table upstairs. Finally, I got it up to the third floor. Now I'm up there, hoping they can't find me—although they keep coming up. But at least I have a space now."

—STUDENT HELEN LOBRANO

"I'm still trying to find a place that's comfortable enough to work. I'm working on the dining room table, but then people come over and I keep putting everything away. So then I took it all to the basement, but it's dark and depressing there. I carry stuff up and I carry stuff down. So now I'm all over."

—STUDENT ANN PORFILIO

Use your dedicated space and scheduled time for homework. Reinforce what you've learned by practicing. Any skill requires repetition to master it. In the case of drawing, apply your skills to subjects that attract you. Practice and record your observations. Take the "drawing mind-set" with you via your small pad and/or by looking at the world through an artist's eyes, observing with drawing in mind.

"I have a space where I can leave my supplies. I draw more if it's ready to go."

—STUDENT SHERRY ARTEMENKO

STORING YOUR SUPPLIES

To protect your work, get an inexpensive portfolio, large enough to hold your largest sheets. If you assemble your supplies in a toolbox or even a cardboard shoe box, you can get all of your pencils, pens, and other supplies out of sight. A card table and chair can provide you with a mobile temporary studio. Searching for the perfect work conditions can be a form of procrastination, so just remember: A drawing can begin with only a piece of paper and a pencil.

Much of what contributes to effective sketching never reaches the paper. Artists routinely preview their activity using a variety of tools to ensure more successful sketching. Previewing allows you to get a feel for what you're going to draw. It's a great help for artists at any level, and particularly anxiety-allaying for beginners who want a practice run before making a mark.

EXERCISE: PRETZEL PREVIEW

You may think this exercise is rather odd, but I assure you, it offers great benefits. So do give it a try.

1 Put a piece of newsprint paper in front of you.

2 Imagine you can see a curvy pretzel on that paper.

3 Looking at that imaginary pretzel, let your eyes actually move as they follow the path of its shape.

4 Your gaze won't flow smoothly. It will feel something like a connect-the-dot exercise as your eye gathers information at points along a shape.

5 Now imagine a straight pretzel stick on your blank paper.

6 Follow that straight line up and down, up and down, creating the shape with the movement of your eyes.

PROJECTED LINES

About how long was your imagined pretzel line? My guess is: short enough to fit on the paper, and that you decided on a top and bottom limit of the line just before you projected it. Try this again, but this time, make it run off the paper. What you are exercising here is the ability to project a line, a skill that will come in handy throughout your drawing experience.

Have you ever noticed how athletes glance over the field, anticipating their moves just before competing? When a concert pianist sits down to play, you may see a similar focused concentration, glances over the keyboard, comparable to the artist projecting an image onto paper. So, exercise this capacity, drawing with your eyes, while you go about your day. It can make ordinary events much more interesting.

PREVIEW TOOLS

We use previewing not only with eye and imagination, but also in actual body movements, calling on our kinesthetic sense. This sense recognizes verticality because we learned to stand upright; the horizontal, because, among other skills, we sign our name on the dotted line. Having moved through space in multiple environments and touched myriad surfaces, our entire body has a stored memory of many life experiences. And again, quite literally, we can draw on this sense as artists.

"I was ready to pitch the drawing of the fluted bowl, but then decided to try and get the general flow of the rim above the one I didn't like. That attempt, although not completed, gave me a sense of the contours and curves."
—STUDENT RITA WALKER COPPING

EXERCISE: GESTURE WRITING YOUR NAME

Use the side of your hand to pretend writing your name in a size that's intentionally too big for your paper. Then reduce the size of your movement as you write, until it fits the paper. You can move your hand above the paper surface or on it to achieve the same result: feeling the shape and scale you intend, without making a mark.

SKETCHING SYMMETRICAL OBJECTS

You don't have to be overly controlled or precise to benefit from these sketching exercises. In fact, you actually give up a little conscious control to do them. Symmetrical objects may seem more difficult to sketch, but they aren't. The simple shapes we work with have no details, nothing to stop the flow of line and movement.

Let's start with the proverbial straight line. Like our preview with the pretzel stick, your aim is to sketch a believable straight line, not a perfect one. When you must have an absolutely straight line, use a ruler; however, a ruler-drawn line in a freehand drawing can look as

out of place as a tux at a barn dance, so it's useful to be able to do a convincing straight line freehand.

Use your piece of paper as a wonderful aid to accuracy: It has four right angles and two sets of perfect parallel lines—horizontals and verticals—to guide you.

Whatever you draw that needs to look vertical or horizontal also needs to be parallel to the sides of your paper. If you want to draw a Leaning Tower of Pisa, your building must tilt away from the sides of the paper. A vertical straight line is parallel to the right and left sides of your paper. If you are drawing an apple, the level place where it sits without rolling will be parallel to the top and bottom horizontals. That doesn't mean the edge of the table itself, just the spot where the apple, or any object, sits without falling over.

EXERCISE: HORIZONTAL AND VERTICAL LINES

Don't draw anything on paper until you reach #3, then use your pencil and newsprint pad.

1 Pencil held in handwriting position, with your hand resting on the paper (left side of paper for righties, right for lefties), move your hand up and down close to the paper edge, over about a 5" distance.

2 Using your imagination, project a vertical line at the paper's edge. Feel the line in the movement of your hand over the paper.

3 When the movement feels right, record it gently with your pencil. Keep recording the movement, going back and forth a few times. Use a crayoning approach to represent the line, as though "filling in" a straight line. If the first few lines are not quite vertical, correct as you go. Think of changing lanes when you drive; you keep moving as you make the adjustment. Your sketched impression of a straight line is in among several lines—it's not just a single line.

This exercise prepares you to sketch convincing, freehand vertical and horizontal straight lines, which are part of many still-life compositions.

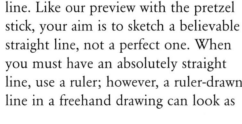

4 Make more horizontals and verticals around the page. For righties, move your hand to the right of the paper's edge to work on the right side of the paper; for lefties, outside the left edge.
5 Add rhythm and a bit of bounce. Your lines will be a composite of two to three overlapping, softly sketched lines.

CONSTRUCTIVE EVALUATION

Stand up and look for a rectangle of negative space made between your line and the paper's edge. Remember that concept? Negative space is created by what is not there as you draw—the empty spaces within a shape or between shapes. If the negative space between your line and the paper's edge isn't a rectangle, then your lines are tilting. Note where your line leans or curves at the ends. Your line may lean right if you're a "rightie," left if a "leftie." Anticipate this tendency and rein in from when you start to curve the line. Practice both lines based on your evaluation. Try some diagonals as well.

EXERCISE: CIRCLES AND LARGER CIRCLES

Don't draw anything on paper until you reach #3, then use your pencil and newsprint paper.
1 Imagine a point visually on your paper.
2 Hold your pencil almost vertically, fingers closer to the pencil point. Make an imaginary circle around this point, with your hand resting on its side and on the knuckle of your pinkie. Gesture some small circles, using multiple swings. (I find counterclockwise more comfortable as a rightie. What works for you?)
3 Now let your pencil point touch the paper and gently record your movement. Keep the movement going around a few times. Add a little pressure when it feels right to do so. If you're judging each circle and feeling insecure, make them all overlap. That

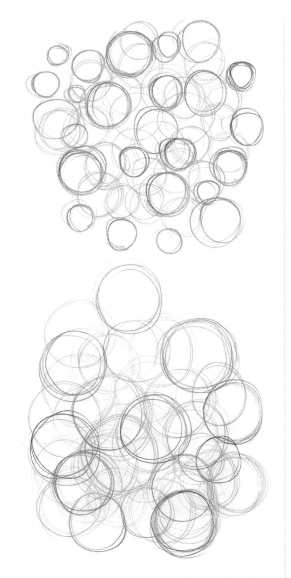

Practicing circles not only loosens your hand; it prepares you to draw myriad rounded objects.

way, you can't see your results as clearly, but can sense them in the swinging movement. Let some circles peek out when they're ready to go public.
4 To create larger circles, move your pencil grip and angle back to normal handwriting position, and use the same technique as above.
5 Put your drawings up on a wall, and study them from a distance. Look at line quality first. Catch yourself now if you're making only one line for each circle. Beginners often think that they'll hit the mark best and be "better" if they can do it perfectly with one swing. Your may see that your circles tilt. Rein in the upswing to correct that tendency. And try this exercise again if you need to do so.

Plumblines and Levels

Ellipses have numerous applications in depicting everyday objects. The lines filled in on the bottom ellipse serve to highlight the unwanted tilt in an ellipse that would need adjustment to appear level.

Two of our accuracy tools take their names from carpentry. The *plumbline* is a vertical dropline: the *level,* a horizontal. We use them to check the accuracy of symmetrical objects. The plumbline will always be parallel to the vertical sides of your paper; the level will be parallel to the horizontal bottom edges.

EXERCISE: ELLIPSE

1 Imagine a flattened circle drawn around a horizontal line.
2 Practice it, recording the movement gently. Bear down a little on your point when it looks convincing.
3 Stand up to look at your work. Draw a level (horizontal) through the sides of your ellipse to check them. If the horizontals look tilted rather than level, your ellipse isn't level.

SEEING AN ELLIPSE

An ellipse is an oval. It can be seen as a circle in perspective. If you hold a cylinder (a round can) in a vertical position, with the top edge at your eye level, you'll see a straight line. As you move the can farther down from eye level, the ellipse appears. It grows more circular the farther away it is from eye level, up or down. Placed on the floor, the top of the can will be a circle when you look straight down at it.

"I always look at my drawings from a distance now, to see whether I've got it placed where I want it, whether it's tilted."

—STUDENT KIM NIGHTINGALE

EXERCISE: CYLINDER

1 To draw a cylinder, start with an ellipse.

2 Draw two verticals, dropped from the sides of the ellipse.

3 Draw the bottom ellipse–the same size as the top one–connected to the verticals.

4 Sketch a vertical line from the middle of the top ellipse to the bottom one. This plumbline allows you to compare right and left sides of the cylinder. If they aren't approximately the same, your cylinder isn't symmetrical. A plumbline and level drawn through your ellipse will be at right angles if your cylinder is vertical and symmetrical.

EXERCISE: BOWL

1 To draw a bowl, start with the top ellipse.

2 Draw vertical plumblines from the center of the top ellipse. The plumbline length determines the depth of the bowl.

3 Sketch a semicircle from side to side of the ellipse. Try to center the greatest bowl depth on the plumbline. Sketching two diagonals from the sides of the ellipse to the plumbline, making a funnel, is a helpful guide to accuracy. Use your plumbline to see if the sides match.

SKETCHING FLUIDLY

Remember to keep pencil and hand close to your paper surface when sketching. Just as in cursive script, each shape will be fluidly connected. Sketching should feel good when your hand gets to move fluidly across the paper's surface.

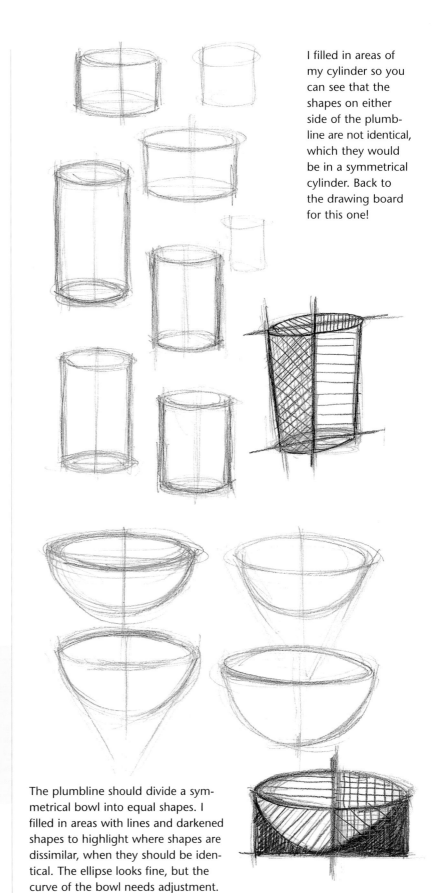

I filled in areas of my cylinder so you can see that the shapes on either side of the plumbline are not identical, which they would be in a symmetrical cylinder. Back to the drawing board for this one!

The plumbline should divide a symmetrical bowl into equal shapes. I filled in areas with lines and darkened shapes to highlight where shapes are dissimilar, when they should be identical. The ellipse looks fine, but the curve of the bowl needs adjustment.

Underdrawing

Underdrawing means just what it says: putting a preliminary drawing under another that will go on top of it. Underdrawing can be employed with any subject, and is especially handy to use as an artistic safety net. For example, all of you who worried about how to avoid drawing curving handles in earlier (Chapter 2) exercises (or how to draw straight handles on tools) will feel more confident about such challenges when you know about underdrawing. To take advantage of this technique, sketch a straight line in pencil as a reference line to guide you when you draw a handle or other symmetrical item, then work right over it with pen, and simply erase your pencil underdrawing afterward.

Apply this sketching technique as accuracy insurance for more complex

Bottles are fun to draw because you stack simple shapes to form them. The label on any curved container will echo the curvature of that surface. Make labels similar in curvature to the bottom or top edge closest to it. You can draw ellipses inside the container to help guide you.

drawings. Lightly sketch the structure of a bowl, bottle, or other object, then check the sketch on a vertical surface for accuracy, to ascertain its symmetry before putting your detailed drawing on top.

EXERCISE: BOTTLE

Bottles, just like people, come in various sizes and shapes. Adapt this basic structure by changing the height of the neck, the width of the base, and so on, as needed. The degree of angle or slope between parts can be changed according to specific bottle contours.

1 Draw a cylinder.
2 Sketch a vertical plumbline through the middle; extend the vertical above the cylinder to double its height.
3 Top the cylinder with an upside-down bowl. The mouth of the bowl and the top ellipse are one and the same.
4 Narrow the cylinder around the top vertical extension, and voilà: You have drawn a wine bottle.

SKETCHING GROUPS OF SYMMETRICAL OBJECTS

Rummage around your home and gather about eight simple symmetrical objects of differing sizes. Recyclables are great, since surface appearance won't figure into this. Cylindrical shapes such as yogurt containers, canned goods, beer bottles, drinking glasses all work; add spheres, such as tennis balls. Make a nice funky grouping.

We use symmetrical objects because their simple shapes make the exercises easier to practice; however, these rules also apply to drawing asymmetrical shapes.

USING YOUR X-RAY VISION

Make a group of three to four objects and place them at an easy viewing distance.

Try for a variety of heights; overlap at least two items slightly. Lightly sketch one item right though the other as though they were made of glass. Don't erase anything; all your lines that search out shapes should show. How do you know what shape to make when you can't see it? Carry through the shape you can see. Just like the carry-through on a baseball swing, start it, then let the momentum carry the line along. Swing through on the curvature of the shape. Carry through along your straight lines.

Beginners tend to contract shapes just before they disappear behind an overlapping shape, as if to squeeze what we can't see back into sight. "Drawing through" helps you to capture the actual shape more accurately, then, for a finished drawing, erase what you don't want to show.

Cylinders of different heights, combined with a sphere, make a good grouping both for practicing drawing symmetrical items and for dealing with the shapes of unseen edges and contours.

These images benefit from the plumbline technique, and most of all, from viewing them at a distance on a vertical surface or wall. It's only from that position that symmetry issues can really be evaluated. STUDENT DRAWINGS, FROM TOP LEFT, BY PAMELA M. HEBERTON, ANITA ST. MARIE, RITA WALKER COPPING

Drawing Asymmetrical Objects

You can use your sketching technique on just about anything now, so scout out some appealing objects from around your home that are not symmetrical.

It's important to work with your small sketchbook (6" × 8" or 8" × 10") now, because on large surfaces, beginners tend to attempt large, time-consuming pieces; the size of the paper seems to call up the "big project," requiring lots of time and diligence. But remember, sketching calls for setting down quick impressions.

After you've collected some interesting, irregular/asymmetrical objects, how should you begin to sketch them?

WRAPPING IT UP

Have you ever received a present wrapped without benefit of a box? Sometimes, but just barely, you can guess what it is. The wrapping usually doesn't reveal any texture or detail.

What if you had to gift wrap each item you've collected individually? What would they look like? Imagine how the wrapping paper would drape over any given shape. Would the contour lines look curved, or all sharply angled? A little of both, depending on what it was draped over, right?

You don't have to see geometric shapes in everything. The idea is to generalize the shape you see in order to begin sketching it. If it translates into a triangular sort of shape, then you've got a handle on something. However, most of the time you'll find a general no-name shape to begin with, because that's the way the organic world happens to look.

EXERCISE: SKETCHING IRREGULAR FORMS

1 Describe the outside shape generally with as few lines as needed to characterize the basic shape, leaving out details, as though the items were within wrapping paper.

2 Look for basic shapes inside the contour. For instance, if you wrapped a tree, some major branches.

3 Develop the contour more now, using smaller broken lines. Give them more specific character.

4 Add a few significant details—as many as needed to suggest the rest without losing the original, informal quality of a sketch. The searching lines of sketching help to give your work movement and interest, so don't censor those searching lines.

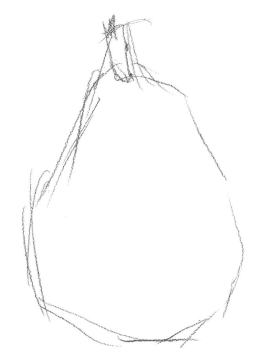

Begin your sketch by characterizing the overall shape of your subject with a gesture of your hand. Then develop the contour with a few loose directional lines to create your basic shape.

DIRECTIONAL LINES

It's easy to get disoriented on a winding path, whether it occurs on your drawing paper or in the woods. Always try to keep the "bigger picture" in mind when drawing its smaller parts. Directional lines are a great tool to help you strengthen your visual compass relative to the entire page, and within the object you're drawing. Breaking complex shapes into smaller, straightish lines also allows you to block them in generally, before putting in curves or detail. So, when drawing wavy, flowing, or rounded shapes:

- *Adapt the wrapping-paper approach to get a general idea where the path is leading and what the overall structure is.*
- *Use long, sketched lines—straightish, but not precise—to characterize the major flow and direction of a bumpy contour.*

Generate your own spontaneous curvy line, and practice using directional lines to characterize it.

Since the hand is a complex shape, it's perfect for practicing the wrapping technique, using directional lines to determine the general change in direction of all the contours.

- *Break down smaller rounded shapes into directional lines in the same way, simply on a smaller scale.*

EXERCISE: WRAPPING YOUR HAND

1 Place your nondrawing hand flat on newsprint paper, and trace it.
2 Sketch around the hand using directional lines, as though you were wrapping it. Your sketch should look like a mitten around your traced hand.
3 Use directional lines to sketch in the semicircular shapes of knuckles.
4 Measure the length of your middle finger against the back of your palm; the relationship is almost equal.
5 Find a reference point for the tip of your thumb against your index finger.

Now is a good time to take some time from reading to sketch. Use your small notebook to keep your sketches casual. Take it with you when you are out and about. When drawing symmetrical objects, begin with a light underdrawing. Check it on a vertical surface, then add a more specific contour sketch on top.

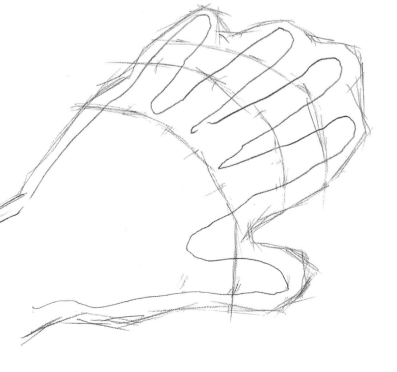

"My sketchbook has become so important. This was a little vase of flowers I drew at Hay Day market while I was waiting for my car to be fixed. The other morning, I drew a plate of scrambled eggs and toast! I've started to do this more—exercising the brain instead of waiting until the kids are asleep and the laundry's done and I've got three hours and I'm not exhausted—because that never happens!"
—STUDENT KATHLEEN LEITAO

47

Additional Accuracy Tools

By now, you've filled your artistic toolbag with a lot of accuracy techniques. It's getting heavy, so why add more? Now that you can sketch groups of objects, *lining up and sighting* are the keys to reproducing their relative placement and proportion with accuracy. Later on, they'll be your most reliable precision tools for drawing the face.

Rectangular objects appear regularly in beginner work, so drawing them accurately is important because a wonderful still-life drawing can be disturbed by a lopsided tabletop. Even without detailed instruction on perspective, a beginner can learn practical ways to draw angles in order to represent them with more confidence.

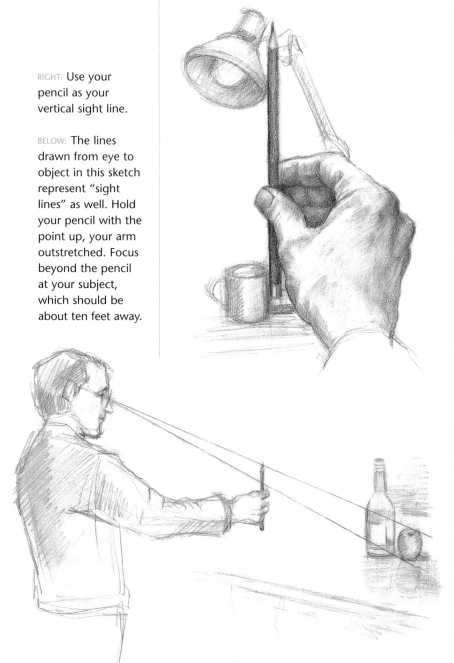

RIGHT: Use your pencil as your vertical sight line.

BELOW: The lines drawn from eye to object in this sketch represent "sight lines" as well. Hold your pencil with the point up, your arm outstretched. Focus beyond the pencil at your subject, which should be about ten feet away.

SIGHTING ESSENTIAL

Always hold your pencil at right angles to the ground during an entire sighting exercise, even if you feel like pointing to the subject as your arm moves up and down.

LINING UP AND SIGHTING TECHNIQUES

Lining up is a variation on the level and plumbline, and is one of the most useful tools at your disposal. It's a technique that helps you record the patterns you see more accurately. Your purpose is to find *two or more reference points that fall along a straight line*. For example, the words on this page are lined up along horizontal lines, and along verticals at the margins, even though these "sight lines" are invisible.

Stand in front of a mirror to find some more ways to sight objects along both level and plumblines. Hold your pencil above your head horizontally, lowering it until it reaches your eyebrows. The tops of both brows fall along a level sightline reinforced by your pencil. Lower it once again to find your earlobes along another level. Hold your pencil vertically to find the vertical sightline between your pupils and sides of your mouth.

Squint while you hold a pencil vertically and scan the room around you. Make sure your head follows the vertical as it moves. Bring the contour edge of the top part of your pencil to the contour edge of another object. Look down the pencil vertical to see if an edge or feature of another shape touches this vertical. Move the pencil around, "sighting" other references. This technique helps you replicate the visual pattern in front of you. Lining up can locate reference points along horizontal and diagonal sight lines as well as vertical ones.

Sighting is a widely used technique for estimating relative sizes accurately. Practice sighting with a partner (or by yourself, if you have a full-length mirror), or use two objects of different sizes, like an apple and a bottle. Align your pencil point with the visible top of your partner's head (or top of the apple). If your partner has big hair, pull the point down a bit to adjust the reading (a bald partner is a plus here). Keep your pencil point in this position while you shimmy your thumb and forefinger down the pencil to a point aligned with your partner's chin (or bottom of the apple). The space between your pencil point and your thumb and forefinger will mark the length of your partner's head, seen from a distance. You now have a unit measuring "one head" (albeit a shrunken one) on your pencil. Keep your fingers in that position on your pencil. Move the pencil point to your partner's chin and count "two heads," and so on. Use that unit to count down the length of your partner's body. You're measuring how many heads high your partner is. A Barbie doll is eight or so; you're doing fine if you come in at six to seven heads.

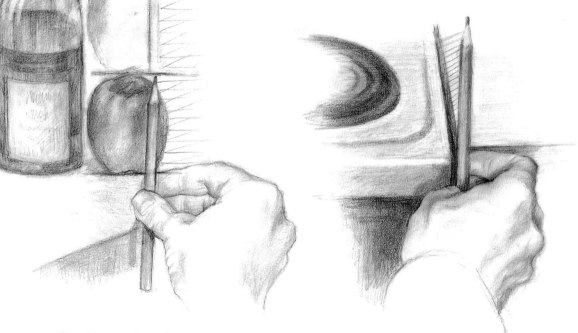

Measure a smaller object against a larger one to determine their size relationship. Here, the bottle is about three apples high. The apple is drawn first, and then the bottle is drawn at a height equivalent to the three stacked apples.

Once again, your plumbline comes in handy. We don't need to worry about verticals and horizontals on the stove; it's the angles at the right and left front stove top corners that we're interested in.

Drawing Angles

Now, let's concentrate on a few techniques that make it easier to draw the angles of rectangular objects. Don't worry if you're geometryphobic! We're not heading for the classroom; we're going to the kitchen. It's a great place to practice drawing angles.

"I found that sketching the horizontal and vertical center lines lightly on the paper, so they could be erased later, helped me a lot in placing my subject in the intended position, not cockeyed."

—STUDENT RITA WALKER COPPING

Stand directly in front of your stove (no less than four feet away) for a nice angle experience. We know the stove top is square, and just like your drawing pad, has four right angles, where perfect horizontals meet perfect verticals. But does it really *look* square? And what's happening to those burners? The parallel sides on the stove top, right and left, seem to turn in slightly toward each other. And the back burners seem closer together than the front ones. Can you see it? Let's test this out.

Squint as you line up your pencil's vertical edge with the stove's right corner. The horizontal edge of the stove should meet your vertical pencil in a right angle (see page 49). Compare your pencil vertical to the right edge of the stove top. This edge will angle slightly away to the left. A triangular wedge of negative space will be created

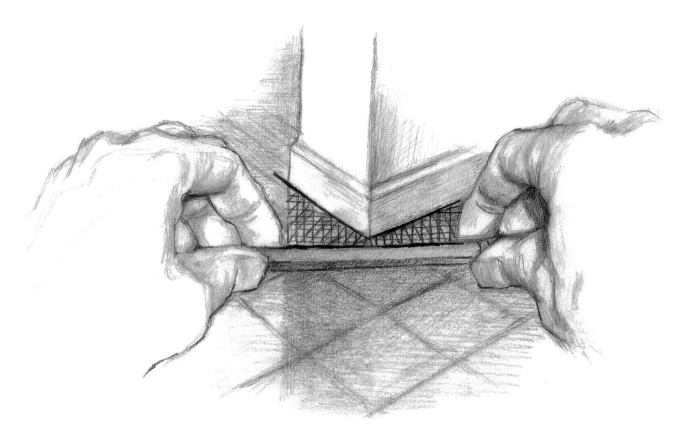

Place your level at a corner to capture negative-space shapes above the level. Look down at a doorway. Place your level under the point where wall and doorjamb meet. The angle of the walls will be seen above the level. Hold your level in two hands, rather than twist it to adapt to the shape. Try sketching these angles. It usually takes some remeasuring and practice, so just keep at it.

between your vertical and the side of the stove. From your vantage point directly in front of the stove, both angles to left and right corners will be the same, each leaning in toward the middle of the stove. What you're seeing is a distortion in parallel lines that causes them to look different from what you know is there. Try sketching these two angles by replicating the wedge of negative space you created, then connect them with a horizontal, and erase your guidelines. Verticals and horizontals don't change, just the angle of the sides of the top. Did you notice that the back edge of the stove looks shorter than the front?

You are the center of your artistic universe! When you change position, the angles do as well. Step to the right past one corner of the stove. Turn your body to face the stove. Remeasure the corner angles of the stove with our plumbline vertical. This time, you will see the negative shapes at both corners forming to the right of your plumbline. The bottom half of these shapes is the angle of the stove top. Are the angles different from one another? Your position is different; so are the angles.

When you are closer to one corner or another, the same angles will not only be different from the first position, but different from each other. When you are directly in front of a rectangular object, angles on the top surface to right and left will be the same.

Remain in this position. Use your level to help you estimate the angle of the front of the stove nearest you. If you have a level longer than your pencil, perhaps a ruler, it will help. The stove front is now at an angle

relative to your body, not lined up with it as it was earlier. Holding the level in both hands at an equal distance from your body, position it just under the stove corner where its front edge and the edge of the stove top nearest you meet. Observe that the stove edge angles slightly up and away from the level to meet the left corner. Assess the negative-space shape captured between this edge and the level. Try to draw the three angles of the stove that you have seen. Draw in the same position from which you measured. Apply this measuring technique to other angles.

> *"We went to a museum with a school trip to look at the dinosaurs. At the end of the trip, the teacher had the class sketch a dinosaur. I was sitting with my daughter, who's not the artist in the family, and I said to her, 'Just look at the individual parts. Look at the head. Is it like a triangle?' And she created this beautiful dinosaur because she was looking at the parts, the shapes, not at the dinosaur."*
>
> —STUDENT STEPHANIE SEIDEL

SELECTIVE VIEWING

Your drawing represents a single view. Even though you focus your eyes on various aspects of the drawing, not everything can be in sharp focus at the same time. You select as though your head and body were stationary and engaged for one sustained look. You don't use information collected by moving around the subject you're drawing, either. Cubism, an art form that melded multiple views into one artistic piece, represents the opposite approach.

Summary

You've been looking at the world as compared with straight lines, whether horizontal (in levels) or vertical (in plumblines). You've done this to collect information and reference points, so that you can draw with greater accuracy. Use these methods to see the overall direction of a curving line or an angle to help you draw, for example, a tabletop. When you project many lines, you create your own graph paper through which to see the world with greater accuracy.

Our aim is not to make engineering or drafting renderings, even when your sketching results in more accurate depictions. Drawing doesn't require that level of precision. Instead, a convincing representation that isn't jarring is the goal. Observe with sighting as an aid; draw, evaluate, then use the measurement tools at your disposal to fix what needs fixing. If you tie yourself up in endless testing and retesting each time, you may squeeze the fun out of sketching.

You've used your sketching line to search for shape and solution rather than declaring an absolute final line. Sketching has its own soft, fluid quality that reflects the time spent in discovering shapes. While it's a tool for increasing your accuracy in drawing symmetrical and assymetrical objects, it's a joy to do and behold on its own.

Your active use of constructive evaluation is a key element in developing accuracy in your work. It gives you a structured approach to ensure ongoing progress. Continue to evaluate to improve, and you'll accelerate your drawing success. When you can identify a problem and apply a solution, it allows you to storehouse more effective tools to apply to your next drawing.

A circle, a cylinder, and ellipses all come into play in this work.
DRAWING BY STUDENT MARGARET R. ADAMS

LOOSE LINES, LOOSE BODY
Sketching to find accuracy actually lets your body relax far more than when you do contour drawing. The lines are loose; your body gets to move more with the sketching line as you flow along with the line. Put on some music that you enjoy to nudge your rhythm along and loosen up your body.

OPPOSITE: *"My daughter Louise had her appendix out. Since I can't sit still and do nothing, I took my sketchpad and pencils to the hospital and worked on this drawing for about four hours while she slept. The fur ball next to her is her favorite stuffed toy—a gorilla she'd had since birth. In a few days, she was fine and back in school. When her classmates saw my drawing, they said all the medical equipment around Louise made her seem small and vulnerable. I hadn't thought about that. I just framed it the way I would a photo."* —STUDENT JIM HOHORST

Homework

Keep your small drawing pad with you and do some sketches during waiting time in a restaurant, in the car when you're picking someone up, and other found-time situations. Try for two to three sketches a week. They don't have to be complete. Sketches can be partially developed impressions and still have charm.

Sketch what interests you, and try to let your line loosen. Incorporate some accuracy techniques along the way. Imagine plumblines and levels even when you aren't drawing. Get into the practice of projecting those lines on the world around you. In effect, draw with your eyes and imagination as you go about your week. It will exercise your ability to discover crucial reference points, which in turn, will increase your ability to observe and create art.

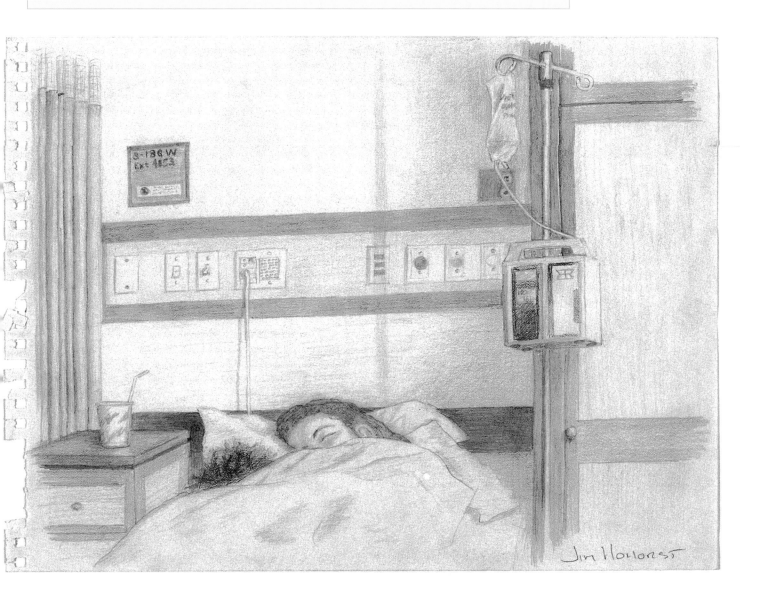

CHAPTER 4

Pencil Values

*"Art is the only way to run away
without actually leaving."*

—TWYLA THARP

SUPPLIES FOR
THIS CHAPTER
2B and 2H pencils
Pink Pearl eraser
14"-x-17" drawing pad
6"-x-8" drawing pad
scrap paper
clip-on light

Now that you can draw recognizable objects with more accuracy, it's time to give them more depth, weight, and substance. To achieve that illusion of three dimensions, you need to add gray tones, also called "values" or "tonal values." These pages will teach you when and how to apply them.

Values are shades of gray, on a scale ranging from black to white. They correspond to how dark or light, in any color, anything appears in the world around you. Beginners initially refer to values as "shading" or "shadowing." If you start to imagine how your surroundings would look in a black-and-white photo, you will begin to "get the picture."

*Value scales are a way of arranging values
systematically, from dark to light. The best way to
distinguish one tone from the next, especially
if they're close in value, is by squinting.*

Values are a significant concept. You'll use a variety of techniques to achieve them in coming chapters, some of which will appeal to you more than others. But in every case, you'll apply them for the same reason: to create the illusion of solidity and spatial dimension.

You'll keep using pencil in this chapter, because it's an ideal tool for creating a full range of gray tones. Pencil serves to fill in the shapes you've been making in the previous chapters with a variety of grays, which correspond to tonal values in anything and everything you may choose to draw.

If you've ever washed a load of laundry, you already know a lot about values. When you separate whites from darks, you're sorting high-contrast values. Colors that fall between darks and lights—beiges, medium blues—belong in the medium-value range. Bright, intense colors need special care. Their intensity doesn't fit easily with other medium colors.

*"When we started
doing the shading,
it all began to
come together.
Now I could make
something that
looked more like it
was supposed to
look in real life."*

—STUDENT PUSHPA
KAPUR

OPPOSITE:

DRAWING BY STUDENT
STEPHANIE SEIDEL

Sorting Out Values

"FINGER PAINTING"

"FINGER PAINTING"

When you smudge, both the movement of your pencil and finger echo the shape of the object you draw. Feel its contours in your imagination, then recreate that impression with the movement of pencil and/or finger. Give yourself permission to do it, to play with it. It's a kind of finger-painting technique that works to create the illusion of an object's surface.

Wherever you're sitting now, check out contrasts in the values around you: books on the shelf, furniture, the markings on your cat, the groceries on your counter. If you're people-watching, notice that each face has its own unique value scheme. Which has the darker value: brunette or blond hair? What about red hair? When you discern that it fits between the two, you've already made a value scale in your mind.

USING HOUSEHOLD ITEMS

Gather seven objects with different solid colors and different values from around your home. Avoid things that are transparent or patterned. A mixture of food, shoes, clothes, and toys will do. Arrange them in a graduated sequence, from darkest to lightest.

SQUINTING HELPS

Close your eyes nearly shut to create a slightly blurred effect. This will eliminate detail and crisp edges, and allow you to focus on the basic, overall value of the objects you've lined up.

It's fun and useful to do this exercise with assistants—kids or adults. Explain the goal and the squint technique. Then take turns placing your collection of objects on a value scale. Just one object per turn, and you can use a turn to correct another's choice.

Two areas will be particularly challenging: Close values are more difficult to distinguish from one another than high-contrast values; and the unique quality of intense colors doesn't translate entirely. They generally fall in the light-to-middle range.

Place objects in the dark and light ends first. Then fill in the middle values, building toward either end. Objects whose values are more difficult to establish will fall in the middle range.

Pick up a problem object and hold it next to each of your other lined-up objects until you find where it belongs. Don't try to get a perfect sequence; just get a feel for the concept for now. There will be natural gaps from one object to the next, depending on the items you've chosen. Some beginners treat these moves like an international chess tournament, until I remind them they're only holding eggplants and lemons!

Leave the items that make up your value scale in place, since you will be referring to them again a bit later.

EXERCISE: VALUE APPLICATION PENCIL SAMPLER

The methods described below create a variety of grays, as in the "Pencil Sampler" (opposite). Refer to those illustrations, but spread yours out much more, use plenty of 14"-×-17" paper, and experiment freely. Notice how we use fine scribbling and other movements that are similar to crayoning. The amount of pressure applied to your pencil point determines how light or dark the values become. Modify results by smudging with your finger or eraser.

1 Test your pencils by scribbling to see their value differences. Drawing pencils with the *H* code have the hardest consistency, and therefore make lighter marks; pencils with the *B* code are much softer, making darker marks.

2 Use your 2B to draw meandering, lazy lines. Let the pressure ebb and flow freely. Lift the pencil and break the line if it feels natural. Notice how the pencil line turns light and dark as it moves, creating *lost and found edges,* also known as *abbreviated contour lines.*

3 Draw six small squares and fill in three with 2B, three with 2H. Fill each square with a different value by controlling pressure: dark, medium, light. Smudge each square; compare the value range.

4 Draw a square. Fill it in with your 2B pencil, making it as dark as you can. Then go over half of the square with your 2H to see how it subdues the 2B texture.

5 Make a series of curved lines, close together.

6 Make a square filled in with horizontal and vertical scribbles.

7 Using your 2B, scribble a coil on your paper. Start with lots of pressure, keeping strokes close together. Ease pressure gradually into middle values, then light ones. Now do the same with your 2H. Erase some of the light end of the first scribbles, then some of the dark. Experiment with both erasers. See which pencil (and which end) is easiest to erase.

8 Make two small triangles, one with 2B, one with 2H. Fill in a value band around each triangle, using the pencil you made them with, respectively. Make the value darker than the triangle contour line. Fill in neatly until the gray band becomes the prominent shape, not the triangle. This is the basis for making convincing highlights; the value of the contour line must merge into the surrounding value. Notice which triangle attracts your eye.

9 Draw a curving line, about three inches long. Then move your hand farther back on the pencil than normal handwriting position. Starting at the line, fill in a one-inch-wide band with a middle-gray value, using long, multidirectional scribbles. The band should bend with the curve of your line. Resume the standard hand position on your pencil. Using more pressure and finer scribbling, build a second, darker band on half of the first, starting right at the line. Add a third, much darker band on half of the second, starting at the line. Create a smooth transition among all

three value areas, using pencil scribbles, eraser, or smudging techniques, so that the bands blend into one another.

CONSTRUCTIVE EVALUATION

Put the "Pencil Sampler" that you created on the wall, and step back. Do you see a variety of gray tones, from extremely dark to very pale, silvery gray? If you didn't make any area really dark, use your 2B to do it now. Keep in mind the full range of gray values at your disposal. Your 2B is the best overall pencil; however, 2H comes in handy for values that are light, silvery, and close, as in light skin or an egg. I often use the two pencils alternately: 2H to sketch in the basic shape and to develop the first value level; then I complete my drawing using 2B with 2H to subdue grainy texture, if needed.

PENCIL SAMPLER. This group of pencil marks shows how to translate the value differences you explored on the opposite page into gray tones with pencil. The various shapes and values of the marks are discussed in the exercise on these two pages.

The illusion of a particular surface is created with pencil strokes. As you examine particular shapes in your sampler, if the surface of your imaginary square looks flat, that is the effect you want. Straight strokes suggest flat surfaces; rounded strokes, a curved surface. Do the values you applied along the meandering contour line evoke roundness? Three values—local, middle (transitional), and shadow—with smooth transitions between them, can make an object appear three-dimensional.

LOCAL VALUE SCALE

Returning to the seven household objects you've lined up into a value scale, make a pencil value scale from them, applying what you learned in your sampler exercises.

Begin by drawing a square to represent each object. Squint and fill in each square with the overall value of its corresponding object. There will be gaps in your scale, as there are gaps in the value range of the objects. However, you should see a gradual change in the squares from light to dark (or vice versa).

ADDING VALUES TO SKETCHES

Find some items that you'd like to draw; use your 14"-×-17" paper. Smooth, rounded objects that have a sculptural quality are best for value studies. Keep them simple. But before drawing anything, let's concentrate on locating and seeing those different value categories.

Put the objects you plan to draw on a plain surface. Illuminate one side of the objects. (Don't use natural light; it moves faster than we can draw.) Turn off additional light sources. Now, see if you can locate these value areas on those objects:

- *Local value is the dominant, overall value of an object, unaffected by shadow or reflections. It relates to an object's position on the value scale, from dark to light. For example, an eggplant has an overall darker value than a lemon, because purple is darker than yellow. The overall value of an eggplant is lighter than the shadow on it. Local value is the lightest of the three important values that make any object appear three-dimensional.*

- *Shadow values are the darkest, found in three broad categories. The first of these:*

- *Shadows on an object are caused by the play of light across it, creating shadows on the side farthest from the light. These shadows are the dark values that give an object its greatest sense of dimension.*

- *Cast shadows, the second group of shadow values, are those that fall from an object to the surface it sits on—in a still life, usually a tabletop—or across the surface of other objects. If you've ever walked down a road at night with the moon or a strong street light behind you, you've*

These illustrations point up overall value (the tomato) and shadows on the objects themselves (the shallots).
DRAWINGS BY STUDENT KIM NIGHTINGALE

seen your own cast shadow. It may become long and distorted, but it's a unique reflection of your shape. If you're out with friends, each shadow can be assigned to each individual, much as it can be to each object on the table in front of you.

- **Balance point shadows,** the third group of shadow shapes, make up the small, very dark area just under an object, where it touches the surface it sits on. Put this shadow value in and it will "ground" your object. Without it, the object will tend to look suspended in space. Balance point and cast shadows give your object a sense of weight.

- **Middle values** provide transition between light and dark value shapes, to create the illusion of dimensionality. Pencil is the perfect medium for replicating that softly blended transitional value. Squinting helps you see shadow shapes. When you can see shadows, it helps you to draw the whole shape, since light and dark puzzle pieces interlock at a common border.

- **Reflected light** can occur as highlight or as lighter areas within a shadow. **Highlights** are areas of reflected light— the brightest spots within light areas of an object. Highlights are often seen as crisp-edged shapes on wet, glossy, smooth, and hard surfaces. In contrast, matte, nonreflective surfaces have light areas, but not highlights. Highlights can be present or not, and are not as crucial as the overall lightest area of the object in creating dimension. Reflected light causes lighter areas within a shadow, but in that case, they are still part of a shadow. Keep them darker than light areas of the object.

STRATEGY FOR DEPICTING HIGHLIGHTS

Highlights on clear glass require a local value of light gray, to provide contrast for the white highlights.

This drawing contains several kinds of shadows. While no highlights are present, notice the reflected light within the shadow on the pumpkin. DRAWING BY STUDENT KIM NIGHTINGALE

A cast shadow of the strawberry echoes its shape, just as highlights reflect varying surfaces of the glass. DRAWINGS BY STUDENT KIM NIGHTINGALE

Basic shapes of objects and shadows are the focus of this casual sketch.
DRAWING BY STUDENT SHERRY ARTEMENKO

SHADOW SKETCHES

Using two or three differently shaped objects from your group, focus on their shadows. Squint to find the specific shadow shapes of each object, concentrating only on cast shadows and shadows on the objects themselves. Make some small, undeveloped "tryout" sketches, and use them just to practice seeing and recording shadow values. Tack them up where you can see them and the subjects, viewing from where you sat to make the drawing. Squint and compare the value shadow shapes.

"I tried to use a 2B for everything, but I found I had a heavy hand, so I had to move to the 2H. What I was trying to achieve using the 2B would turn out to be much too dark."

—STUDENT RITA WALKER COPPING

"I did a drawing before of a squash and it wasn't so good, but then I did this, and I thought, boy, this is pretty good! From that point, it felt do-able. I thought it would be dull and boring with no color, but it had lots of character." —STUDENT PUSHPA KAPUR

Pressure on the 2B pencil yields the darker value scale and bold impact we see in this tulip arrangement. DRAWING BY STUDENT PAMELA M. HEBERTON

The silvery tonal values in this floral reflect a light touch with the 2B pencil. DRAWING BY STUDENT GENIE BOURNE

Step-by-Step Value Drawing

Art is created in layers. We begin with an underdrawing, then work on top of it in steps, as in this demonstration. Darker values, crisper contours, and more details are added gradually. Every stage is a blend of steps, including back steps to erase, or a jump ahead, to add values before the final step. Focus on an object from your group that particularly appeals to you—one you are willing to spend time with. Point a light on the object to bring out more dramatic dimension. Use 14"-×-17" paper, 2B and 2H pencils, and the eraser on a writing pencil.

STRATEGIES FOR FILLING IN OVERALL VALUE

When you fill in an object's overall value, change the direction of your strokes every cluster or so. Keep the shape of the object in mind to direct your scribble in directions that suggest the object's contours. Try to identify at least two directions of the surface— for instance, up and down and around— and move your pencil in those directions to fill in value. Don't flatten a rounded object by applying straight lines in one direction only. Smudge to finger-paint the surface of the object with the pencil dust.

CONSTRUCTIVE EVALUATION

Compare your subject matter with your drawing, viewed at a distance. Do you see anything that needs fixing? Squint hard to pick up on any value areas that need attention. Ask yourself:

- *Are my value shapes accurate?*
- *Is a degree of dimension emerging?*
- *Do my value edges transition softly where necessary?*

If your answer is *yes* to any of the above, you're well on your way. Now you have something to build on.

STEP 1: UNDERDRAWING. Use your preview tools and a light sketch to indicate the basic shape and scale of the object. If you're working with a symmetrical object, check it out on a vertical surface at viewing distance.

STEP 2: DEVELOPING FEATURES. Work on contours and add detail. Lightly outline any highlights. Establish the local value with a base of long, flattish scribbles. If your object is very light, use a 2H; otherwise, a 2B. Stay in the middle-value range for this step, no matter what your subject. Add the shadow shape on the object, always darker than the overall value. Soften the transition between shadow and overall value by using less pressure on your pencil. Put in the cast shadow, incorporating horizontal strokes to help the shadow lie flat. Show reflected light in the shadow, either by erasing shadow values or darkening around them. Ground the object with a balance-point shadow just beneath the object where it touches the surface.

STEP 3: FINALIZING. Look at your sketch carefully, squinting to check out values as compared with subject matter. Then overlay the base with shorter, tighter scribbling, changing direction often over all value areas. Use your eraser or finger to smooth out texture; your pencil point to make crisp, sharp edges and darker values where needed. Develop highlights and don't let the highlight outline stay darker than the surrounding value. Let the white of the paper represent the brightest highlights in your drawing. Some highlights may be darker than the paper. As a final touch, if the highlight has a soft edge, use your eraser to blur it.

Problem Solvers

Problems routinely occur in art and in life. We feel better about making so-called mistakes if we not only acquire the ability to spot a problem, but also learn how to fix it. Although we have worked only with pencil and pen so far, the following common problems and helpful solutions apply to all value drawings—not only with pencil and pen, but with wash, charcoal, and Conté, all of which will be introduced in later chapters.

PROBLEM. Is the cast shadow on your tabletop too active, too contoured?

SOLUTION. Horizontal strokes within the shadow will flatten it, thereby reinforcing the flat table surface.

PROBLEM. Are the highlights on your drawing vague, not convincing as the brightest parts of the object?

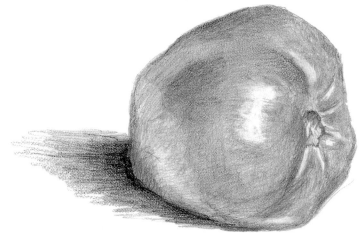

SOLUTION. Camouflage the outlines around highlights, and make them pop up well, with an application of darker, finer value scribbles.

PROBLEM. Does the shape look flat, with an abrupt transition between values, making the shadows seem pasted on, not integrated into the drawing?

SOLUTION. Overlay stacks of straight lines with multidimensional strokes; use transitional grays between shadow and overall value; soften with finger or eraser.

PROBLEM. Does the shape look somewhat flat, not convincing the viewer that it's a three-dimensional object?
DRAWING BY STUDENT STEPHANIE SEIDEL

SOLUTION. Use more values to create dimension. Darken the lower portion of the object, where it begins to merge with a shadow. DRAWING BY STUDENT STEPHANIE SEIDEL

PROBLEM. Is your contour line too dominant in relation to the object's overall value?

SOLUTION. If you have drawn your contour line with uniform pressure, create "lost and found edges" by softening the contour here and there with your eraser.

PROBLEM. Does your object seem to float rather than sit solidly on a surface?

SOLUTION. Add the small, dark shadow shape beneath the object to ground it to the table.

PROBLEM. Is the object too pale, as though it's fading away?

SOLUTION. Reinforce contours here and there and add darker shadows.

PROBLEM. Have you focused more on surface pattern than on depicting dimension, thereby causing the pattern to look flat?

SOLUTION. The entire object, including surface pattern, should show the effects of light and shadow in order to achieve a three-dimensional look.

67

Banish Perfectionism

Added to the series of "Problem Solvers" just presented, here's one more: *Problem:* Being too critical, expecting perfection. *Solution:* Every time you worry about whether you have talent, whether you're "good enough," banish those thoughts and just keep drawing!

"I decided to just let go and surrender to what came out. I found that when I did let go and just draw, I became so absorbed in the work that I wasn't thinking about anything else. It was like a meditative state. I had found a place where I could shut out all other things and just be. It was a peaceful feeling."
—STUDENT ANITA ST. MARIE

Fear that you don't have talent is often based on a belief that a piece of art needs to be perfect, that *you* need to be perfect. None of us can achieve perfection. In fact, when what you consider imperfect comes through in your drawing, that may be just the part that has your personal stamp and makes it unique to you. That is often where the art is.

Just concentrate when you work, learn from what you do, but don't treat any one drawing as though it's the culmination of everything you hope to do. It's just one drawing; many more empty pages are waiting to give you many more drawing experiences.

"I let go of having to get it perfect. This was just for me, because I enjoyed doing it. I released myself from proving anything."
—STUDENT ANGELA LOWY

Beginning artists will have a moment when they finally understand that wonderful art is not perfect technique or a perfect replication of subject matter. Cameras can do that. It's the individual's take on what is seen, that personal filter through which reality is perceived, that makes drawings or any art form authentically beautiful, or potentially so. That truth has been recognized throughout the history of art. Perfectionism hobbles our energies. We are afraid of being seen for who we are, afraid of being vulnerable. But making art requires the courage to permit yourself to be yourself.

In my teaching experience, it's never been the student with the greatest initial drawing ease that develops the most. A combination of intense interest and a flexible learning attitude seems to ensure the most positive development. The ability to learn from the drawing experience, and to shrug off a disappointing result, is a definite accelerator.

"A strong perfectionist bent had prevented me from trying anything I might not be good at. I learned to risk failure, because there was such pleasure in producing small drawings."
—STUDENT ANN PORFILIO

SHOW AND TELL—OR DON'T

Beginners in my classes thrive on the "show and tell" period, a structured evaluation of homework drawing that's part of every session. However, when working on your own with this book, you may choose not to share your drawings with others. Some like to show their work to everyone immediately, while others prefer to keep it private. Do what feels best for you. And be aware that people who have not been exposed to the art world or art instruction may feel awkward in discussing your work—so *you* may have to do some teaching before sharing your drawings with them!

EXERCISE: CLOSE AT HAND

Here's a variation on our earlier draw-your-hand exercise. It's a fun way to get to exercise your pencil, observe proportions within your hand, and learn a bit about skin tone. Use your 2B or 2H pencil, depending on which matches your skin value more closely: 2B, the softer pencil, will make darker tones; 2H, the harder pencil, lighter tones. After you've completed this exercise, try sketching your hand in a variety of positions.

1 Trace your nondrawing hand, palm down, fingers together or spread. Draw the folds in your knuckles.
2 Put in shadow shapes if they are present, squinting to see them.
3 Use contour drawing to fill in specific nail shapes.
4 Fill in an overall skin value and use your finger to smooth out the surface. Use your directional lines to map out rows of knuckles in a slight semicircle.

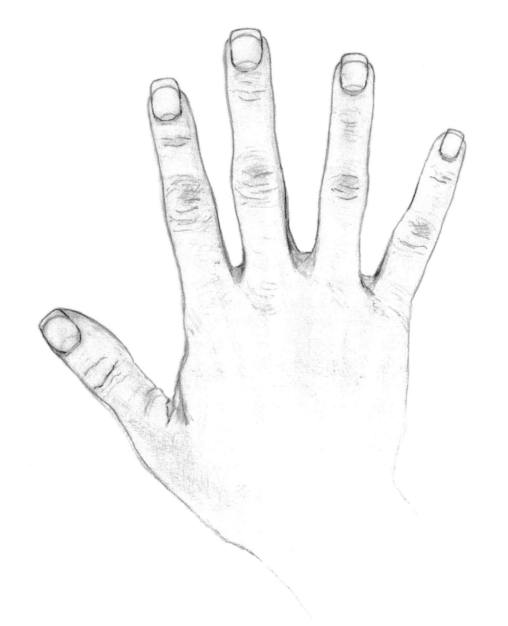

"When I did my hand, I searched for light and dark lines, thin and thick lines, and went back again and again until I got it right—for me. When I got to drawing the tendons in my hand, I found that dragging the eraser gave it new dimension. I was immersed in the patterns of lines that became my knuckles, and the half moons that were created by my cuticles. I must have spent at least six hours 'fixing' my hand, but I loved every minute!"
—STUDENT KRISTEN NIMR

69

Studies

As you add values to your sketches, they will gain a sense of dimension and weight. They may look less like fleeting impressions and more like solid objects, especially at a distance. The more time you spend adding visual information to your drawing, the closer you get to creating a study. The name itself implies that the artist has spent time closely observing the object, often a single object. This scrutiny may result in more substantial, solid-looking drawings, with more detail and refined technique. The major differences between sketch and study are that in creating a study, more time is spent at a slower pace, adding a greater amount of detail, with more refined value application.

STRATEGY FOR HIDING PENCIL STROKES

This is a refinement of scribbling, used where you want few discernible pencil strokes to show. It's easiest to achieve with a 2H pencil. Hold it loosely, with the point barely touching the paper, exerting no pressure as you make a soft gray value by jiggling the pencil gently. Change the direction of your application further by letting your elbow rise and fall from your side as you work.

TAKE YOUR TIME

Many beginners wonder if they're taking too long. It's not how long *you* take; it's how long the *drawing* takes. Just stay with it until it feels and looks finished—to you.

If your sketches are developing into studies, or you'd like them to, add the following points to your drawing approach. For creating a study:

- *Slow your pace.*
- *Break up contour lines into smaller overlapping lines.*
- *Keep your pencil in closer contact with the paper surface.*
- *Fill in values with greater precision.*
- *Add more detail.*
- *Evaluate each area more frequently.*

The many different values shown here turn even a simple subject like this eraser into an interesting picture. DRAWING BY STUDENT MARGARET R. ADAMS

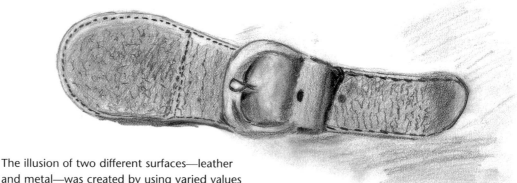

The illusion of two different surfaces—leather and metal—was created by using varied values and pencil strokes. DRAWING BY STUDENT ANGELA LOWY

Deep folds and subtle creases turn a humble paper bag into an ideal subject for a pencil study with a wide value range. DRAWING BY STUDENT JANE WOLANSKY

This ball of string, or any sphere, takes on roundness when dark-to-light values are added to express three-dimensionality. DRAWING BY STUDENT LUCIA MOTTA-SILVA

"I had to do some homework for class, so I grabbed a water bottle as I was running out of the house, put it on a glass table by the pool, and drew while the kids swam—then went to many other places, drawing when I could. I didn't go back and change it, didn't have any high expectations. I just wanted to do my homework and make some progress." —STUDENT PAMELA SHILLING

Homework

Make studies and sketches, with and without values, and do lots of try-outs—just to see what happens. Continue to be on the lookout for subject matter that engages your interest and gives you the urge to draw.

"I had zilch training when I started the course. I began the mushroom in class, and it was so detailed, I was a bit scared, but became completely engrossed. We'd been taught to step back every so often, and I realized I'd been sitting there for long without doing that. I was shocked when I stood back, and all the pieces matched up. Usually, things don't match up, and I have a lot of erasing to do. But the fact that the contour drawing joined up gave me confidence. I took the mushroom home, and got more engrossed in the detail. I thought I'd been working for about a half hour, but it was about three hours!"
—STUDENT HELEN LOBRANO

"I eliminated detail by squinting and just saw the shapes. It was really fun, the most fun. I just let myself go." —STUDENT ANNE BALLANTYNE

One of the pleasures of drawing is that there's always something close at hand—or at foot—to serve as your model. DRAWING BY STUDENT PAMELA SHILLING

Expanding Value Technique: Wash, Pen, Pencil

"We must . . . give the image of what we actually see, forgetting everything that has been seen before."

—PAUL CÉZANNE

It's so satisfying to expand drawing technique with the addition of just one new ingredient: *wash*. You can use wash to accent a drawing, create a wider range of values, and add a graceful, fluid look to your work.

What is a wash? Essentially, it's tinted water, made by mixing a small amount of paint with a larger amount of water. A wash is transparent; you can see the texture of your drawing surface through it. Washes are the basis of the painting technique used by watercolorists.

When applying a wash, your brush should glide over the paper surface. If it pulls on you, your brush is too dry; give it more water.

You'll create and apply washes with your brush. It can be an inexpensive watercolor or acrylic brush; just make sure it comes to a crisp point. Although I specify a "round" brush (in "Supplies," page 11), be aware that some brushes classified as rounds will not make the crisp point that you'll need to get into nooks and crannies with good control, so shop carefully.

Once you've made your choice, be nice to your brush; it will last longer with some basic tender care. Never leave it full of paint or wash. Keep it in water, hairs down, while working—but don't leave it that way for a prolonged period, or the hairs will curve. (If you forget and that does happen, dip the end in boiling water for a second or two to reshape hairs.) Wash brushes after each use with warm water and mild soap, then leave them lying flat or in a jar to dry, hairs up.

SUPPLIES FOR THIS CHAPTER

2B and 2H pencil
2 drawing pens, fine and micro nibs
black watercolor paint
6"-×-8" drawing pad
14"-×-17" drawing pad
Pink Pearl eraser or writing-pencil eraser
disposable palette
water jar
#6 brush
facial tissues
tape
Q-Tips

"I'd been taking a watercolor class and was frustrated because I didn't draw, and I needed to remedy that."
—STUDENT REGINA BRAUER

OPPOSITE:

DRAWING BY STUDENT JANE WOLANSKY

Creating a Wash

Previewing values
is key to a good
experience using
wash. Washes dry
out, therefore when
you mix them, have
a fairly clear objec-
tive about where
you're putting them.
Anticipate your
move, then be ready
to pop the wash in
where you want it.
Always preview first,
make your wash,
then go!

*Wet flows into wet;
let it dry
and it will set.
(My poem for you!)*

Before we make a wash sampler, let's concentrate on making a wash. First, place all your supplies on the table on your drawing-hand side, with your water jar filled. Squeeze a one-inch line of the black paint on your palette. If you're using freezer paper as your palette, tape it down so it won't curl up. About a 12" square piece is a good size.

If your brush is brand-new, it will be stiff with a gel-like coating, which can be removed by pushing the brush firmly against the bottom of the jar, then shaking it around in the water. Notice how the brush hairs hold water when you lift it out, dripping a bit here and there. If it's too drippy, draw the hairs gently across the jar's edge to remove excess.

With your brush, pull off a small amount of pigment from the edge of your paint, not from the middle.

Mix water and paint together, making a puddle on your disposable palette. Since plastic won't absorb liquid, the puddle will contract on the freezer paper or plastic plate, saving the paint for your work. However, you can't see the value you've created clearly until you test the wash on scrap paper. Do that now.

To dilute the paint and lighten its value further, add more water to the paint that's still on your brush. Just dip the brush in water again. Continue dipping to add more water to the original paint on your brush, and test each time by dabbing on your paper. Since you're adding more water, never more paint, the proportion of water to paint is increased with each dip, diluting the mixture gradually and lightening its value from black to palest gray. Test after each dip, and you'll have a record of many different values on your paper.

EXERCISE: WASH SAMPLER
With this, and with samplers in all chapters, refer to illustrations, but use as much paper as you need. Keep your drawings to about a half-sheet or smaller from your 14"-×-17" pad, or use your 6"-×-8" pad. Feel free to experiment with the techniques presented, but note that drawing paper is not always meant for entire paintings created with wet media. If you use too much wash, the paper will buckle. Remember: Your washes are meant to be used only as complements to drawing. As for your #6 brush, it is suited to smaller images, like those in this exercise (and through-out the chapter); large areas call for larger brushes. If you use a smaller brush with many small strokes to cover a large area, streaks will result.

1 Make a wash with enough water to get a transparent puddle.

2 Test the wash value on scrap paper. Add more water to the wash on your brush to change value. Repeat this process, testing your results each time until you create a light wash.

3 Make a stroke of pale wash on your drawing paper. Let it dry; we'll come back to it later.

4 Make a little group of dots with your point.

5 Create a range of pencil values clustered together on the page. Then put a light wash over them. The wash adds a unifying smooth gray, while the pencil adds complex values through the transparent gray.

6 With the point of your wash-filled brush, make a dark stroke of wash. Blot immediately with a tissue; it makes a fine eraser.

7 To make a crisp edge along a wash line, draw a vertical pencil line (about two inches long). Position your wash-filled brush point up and parallel to the line. Press the point gently down and onto the paper until the hairs fan out, touching the vertical line on one side. You'll be creating the crisp edge with the side of your brush, not the point. Pull the brush toward you along the line. If the wash runs out, turn the brush over to replenish, and keep going. This is a more efficient technique than using the brush point to paint along a straight edge. Try the same thing along a curved line.

8 Put two wash strokes next to each other, overlapping edges slightly, to see how one flows into the other.

9 Make a stroke of wash, then immediately add clear water to its edge. Clear water draws the wash toward it, softening the setting edge.

10 Make a stroke of wash. Use the brush point in small, feathering flicks to break up the a setting edge.

11 Create some small white shapes—such as a triangle, a heart—by painting around them. Make the darkest wash you can without losing transparency.

12 Make several small rectangles in pencil. Create a wash. Prop your pad up at a slight tilt. (Either hold it with a free hand, or better, prop it up on something.) Add a stroke of wash at the top of the rectangle. Add another stroke immediately beneath it, overlapping its edge. Continue down the page, feeding wash to each stroke edge before it sets. Gravity helps the wash travel, so tilt your pad more, if necessary, to help it along. You may accumulate unwanted wash at the bottom of a rectangle. Keep the pad tilted to avoid backwash. Dip a Q-Tip into excess wash to absorb it. Twist the corner of a tissue into a wick to do the same.

13 Continue tilting your paper for this exercise. Make an irregular shape. Moisten it with water. Add wash to the premoistened shape and watch it travel. You can add more wash and nudge it along, but don't stroke.

14 Using the pale wash that you set down to dry earlier (Step 3), cross over that stroke two times. You should see a darker value at the crossover.

HOW TO SOFTEN A DRY, SHARP EDGE

Any wash edge will "set" in a fixed position with a sharply defined edge if you brush it on and leave it alone to dry. To soften a dry edge, rub gently with a wet brush or Q-Tip.

WASH SAMPLER. The wash applications shown here are described in the exercise that begins on the opposite page. Refer to these examples in building your own "Wash Sampler."

EXERCISE: PENCIL STUDIES
WITH WASH

Use your 6"-×-8" pad, or put two or three studies on your larger paper. Choose some objects you'd like to draw. We've had nice results with mushrooms, shells, tulips, teacups—all small objects with close, light values. Pencil and wash studies have an intimate look; quiet and subdued because of their light values.

Flowers, fruit, and a humble scrub brush make equally appealing still-life subjects. STUDENT DRAWINGS, FROM TOP, BY PAMELA SHILLING (LILY), MARY E. TANGNEY (LEAF, BRUSH), AND SHERRY ARTEMENKO (APPLE, PEPPER, BANANA)

1 Select one object (your beloved!), and place it close to you if you'd like to see details more clearly. Building on what you've already learned, begin with a pencil study and complete all value areas, including cast shadows.

2 Make the lightest wash possible. Stay with this value throughout this exercise. Your value patterns are now set by the pencil and will be visible through the transparent wash, which will be an accent. Remember, the keys to success in adding wash in this exercise are: Be ready to soften edges if necessary; use only the same light wash.

3 Test your puddle of wash. If it's dried out or becomes more concentrated, you may need to mix more. Keep it very light. Don't use an overloaded brush. If it goes too dark or you get a flood, blot with a tissue immediately.

4 Apply a very light wash over your entire study, except for highlights. Since the wash is transparent, your underlying pencil work will provide a variety of visible values. Washes give a soft connecting gray value to everything. Where an application looks fine, don't keep going around that area.

5 Move your brush with the flow of your object's surface, as though you were a small bobsled traveling over its hills and valleys. Move with purpose and get out quickly once you've done the job. If you're already getting streaks, add more water to your wash.

6 While your wash is wet, you can add more of the same light value; not more paint, just wash—over painted areas to deepen a value.

7 To keep a crisp edge, let it set before putting wash next to it, since wet flows into wet. Edges will set if you leave them alone to dry. Defining crisp edges is especially helpful in strengthening your art.

8 Let your picture dry for a few minutes. Surfaces will be cool to the touch while

wet; slightly warm when dry. Once your drawing is dribble proof, put it up on the wall, then sit down with your subject between you and your picture. Use the same criteria for critiquing this as for any value drawing.

9 Try this exercise more than once. The first time familiarizes you with the materials and how they work; the second time, you can be more relaxed.

CONSTRUCTIVE EVALUATION

Is there any additional detail you notice that can be added to bring out dimension? You can't erase, since the wash seals in the surface pencil work. However, you can deepen dark values and define edges with some wash or pencil. Add pencil only when your picture is totally dry, to avoid tearing the paper. Wash can also be added immediately after a previous wash was applied. But adding more wash while it's drying can lift the previous wash. There's a limit to the amount of layering your paper will take.

WHAT IF IT DOESN'T COME OUT?

The drawings by beginners shown here are examples of what works. For every success, there are many drawings that aren't as strong. As one beginner describes it, "Sometimes I put a line up there and I knew it wasn't right (and I was right). Yet, other times, it all added up and the time just flew by." Be tolerant of your not-so-successful drawings. They're all part of the process that brings forth the special ones. Keep them all so you'll have a record of your progress.

But if you're really frustrated dealing with a drawing that doesn't please you, take a break. Frustration and disappointment are natural parts of the learning process. With drawing, it doesn't help to be a slave to the art. Back off when you must, have a coffee or tea or take a walk—then return refreshed, and begin again.

Even something as simple as a curve of ribbon can make interesting subject matter. DRAWING BY STUDENT NANCY OPGAARD

"I wanted to draw a peanut, a bell, and other basic shapes [apple, egg, block]. The pattern/texture of the peanut and the exotic nature of the antique bell are what attracted me to them. As to placement on the pages, they just fit. No pressure, just fun!" —STUDENT MICHELLE G. CAPPELLIERI

Pen Techniques

Let's concentrate on pen now, to take your skills to another level. You can sketch with a pen using a technique similar to the one employed with pencil. Begin by observing the contours of objects, both inside and out. Then, when you commit those contours to line, break them up naturally and spontaneously.

Pen values are created through three basic techniques:

- **hatching:** *making a series of closely set parallel lines;*
- **crosshatching:** *making sets of close, parallel lines crossed over one another, usually at right angles, either casually or in a more controlled way;*
- **stippling:** *making a group of small dots, dabs, or other tiny marks to produce a dappled effect.*

Let's do some exercises to get a feeling for these useful techniques.

"I would force myself to just jump in, follow the lines, and keep going—not let myself look at it until the end. That somehow helped me to get over my fear of not being able to draw realistically."

—STUDENT TRACEY M. ROBINSON

EXERCISE: PEN SAMPLER

Pen values are created by reducing or expanding the spaces between marks. The closer the marks, the darker the values. Although pressure can produce somewhat darker marks, reducing the space between them is the key.

1 Working on your 14"-×-17" pad, begin by testing both your micro and fine pen nibs with scribbles to see their different value ranges.

2 Fill the bottom of your page with some flowing, squiggly, angular, ribbony strokes, anything you can think of to fill space in spontaneous ways. Make little marks or long, continuous lines that look like imaginary handwriting—whatever comes out.

3 Make a scribble with each pen, starting with very close, very tight coils, then make them looser, farther apart at the end. Your values will move from dark to lighter in tone.

4 Draw three squares. Fill the first with vertical strokes, leaving obvious spaces among them. Make strokes closer together each time. As spaces contract, you need more strokes to fill the same size square, and the squares get darker. Make lots of these. Play with this until it feels quick and automatic.

5 Do the same with horizontal strokes. To get into the repetition, do it quickly. And listen to the sound your pen makes. There's a real rhythm to it. You can hear the number of strokes and the speed increase together. Faster, closer strokes often seem easiest.

6 Overlap vertical and horizontal lines, keeping the space between them approximately the same. Add a row of diagonals.

7 Make a square as dark as you can with lots of fast, close strokes. Use diagonals as well.

8 Outline two small squares and fill them with small marks. Use dots for the first, then any marks you want for the second. As noted earlier, stippling is a way to create values out of small dots, but you can also make up your own tiny marks to create a dappled pattern. The amount of space between marks creates value changes. Try making the corner of each square a darker value.

9 Make a coil, rhythmically and quickly done, and let it spiral into an increasingly narrow coil, like a tornado. Build up your energy with a quick practice coil gestured above the paper before you begin. Make lots of them!

10 "Mole holes" is the nickname used in my classroom for marks that are almost semicircles. They also look a bit like croquet wickets. Do them rapidly, automatic-pilot style. Listen for the sound of the quick marks. Don't over-control. You begin to feel the centrifugal pull as your hand whips around the shape and comes to a stop.

11 Notice the small value hatches along tornadoes and mole-hole shapes. They reflect the same curvature as the associated larger shape, but are not as wide. You'll apply these small hatches in a column down each side of the larger shapes, starting each hatch on the outside of the larger shape and moving toward the middle. Then make a narrower column on top of that. You can add one small column at the edges to increase dimensionality more. Figure out where you're going, then put your hand on automatic pilot and start in. A rapid approach works better than a slow one.

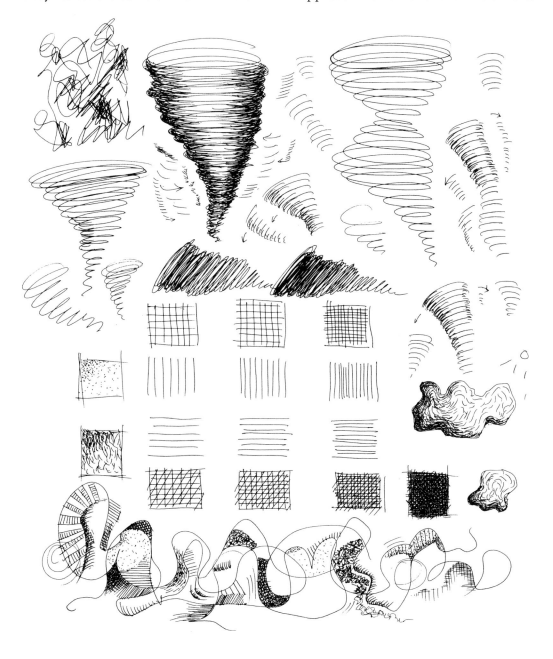

PEN SAMPLER. Refer to these marks in constructing your own "Pen Sampler," as described in the exercise that begins on the opposite page.

STRATEGIES FOR DRAWING WITH PEN

• Don't strive for perfection in each stroke. It's the overall accumulation that counts. Have fun and let 'er rip!

• Have your pen strokes mimic the shape of the object, just as you did with pencil. Let your pen move in more than one direction. Crossing over your strokes in another direction helps create a three-dimensional effect. If a cylinder is both round and tall, use strokes in both directions.

• Make crosshatching quickly. Don't pull marks with your whole arm; let your hand and fingers do the work.

Potential subject matter for pen drawings is all around us. Select what catches your eye. STUDENT DRAWINGS, FROM TOP CLOCKWISE, BY MARY JO FUSARO (PLANT, BOTTLE), MICHELLE G. CAPPELLIERI (PULLEY), AND ANNE OSSO PORCO (SPRAY VALVES, MORTAR AND PESTLE, TOOL)

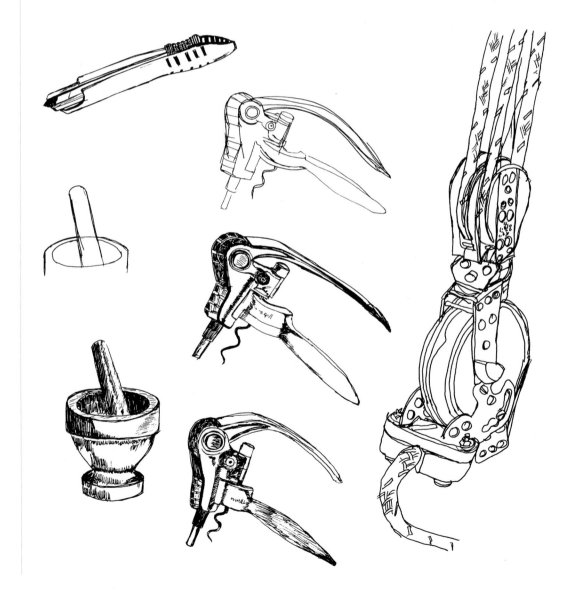

As you probably noticed from the examples shown on earlier pages, shoes have been a popular subject in my classrooms, for both pencil and pen drawings. STUDENT DRAWINGS, FROM TOP CLOCKWISE, BY JANE WOLANSKY (SNEAKER), TRICIA VANACORE (SKATE), PAMELA MCFEELY (SLINGBACK), AND M. E. OLSON (SANDAL)

"I thought about things I would do when I got the time. At the top of my wish list was learning to draw. It was time to move to something that gave some space to the soul." —STUDENT AL ROBERTS

EXERCISE: ROUNDED/ IRREGULAR SHAPES SAMPLER

What about hatching rounded or irregular shapes? The technique is similar to the loose movements used in sketching. Work on a sheet from your smaller drawing pad, using both pens for this two-step exercise.

1 Make a small, freeform shape. Fill it with dashes that mimic the contour shape, as though your strokes described streams of water, flowing over rock.

2 Make a similar shape. Fill it in again, but this time, make one side of the shape darker than the other by filling in the spaces between marks. See if you can make a clear value transition by gradually decreasing white spaces.

These two drawings match subject matter effectively with the contrasting qualities inherent in pencil and wash, and the more assertive nature of pen and wash. DRAWINGS BY STUDENT ANNE OSSO PORCO

Adding Pen to Pencil and Wash

Layering pencil, pen, and wash yields a more assertive result than pencil and wash, since the black pen line is definitive, bold, and high contrast. The approach is similar to using pencil and wash. However, your pencil drawing is used as a safety net, rather than for values. Pen offers both contour and value. Light wash is added to provide a unifying middle gray. Reapplication of both wash and pen deepens values. Crisp and soft edges need attention. Constructive critique helps you see where darker values and edge work is needed.

Choose subject matter that you enjoyed using for contour drawing. Your pen line is best for boldly defined, detailed objects with clear edges and segments, as opposed to a simple rounded object like an egg. Work with items that excite you, but also have definite, rather than suggested, edges.

*"You need to think, It's only art.
My feelings are important here!
Anger can break the negative connection.
It's like: I'm in charge!"*

—STUDENT ISABEL TORBERT

Try marks like these to see how adding pen to pencil and wash can enhance a drawing.

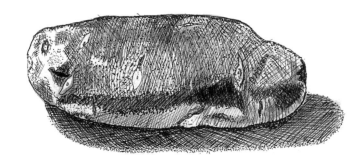

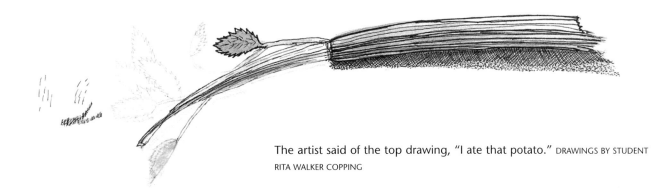

The artist said of the top drawing, "I ate that potato." DRAWINGS BY STUDENT RITA WALKER COPPING

85

Using Pencil with Pen and Wash

Begin with a pencil underdrawing, applied according to the effect you want. Applying pencil first will increase your technical control before you add ink and wash.

Your pencil underdrawing can be:
- *a simple vertical or diagonal guideline to give a tool or upright object a straight reference;*
- *a general sketch to help control scale and placement of the object on your page, as well as give you a preliminary feel for that object;*
- *a complete, detailed drawing.*

In a casual drawing, retain your pencil marks if you like the look. With a formal pen drawing, erase your pencil underdrawing (no one will know you had a safety net) after the ink is dry.

"I used to rip up all my drawings. I don't have any of that early work, and I'm really sad about that. I could have learned a lot of things if I had kept them. Now, I put my drawings away for a while. Sometime I take out a drawing that I do like and put it up on a wall and think, I did something that was O.K.! That helps."
—STUDENT SUSAN PARSONS

Once your pencil line is in, do your pen drawing, putting in as much texture and detail as you want. You can sketch with pen, using a spontaneous, intuitive approach. Values can be filled in with quick marks, or even scribbles, that describe the surface. A more formal approach simply means more precision. *Micro* pen nibs create a finer mesh of marks that are less pronounced than the *fine* nib makes. Outlines work best with the fine nib; shadow areas are more effective with the micro. Washes over pen lines can subdue their bold look, as well.

Wash application echoes the movement of leaf surfaces in these eloquent drawings. Darker layers result from a buildup of light, transparent values.
FROM TOP, DRAWINGS BY STUDENTS LINDA FITZGERALD AND ANN BALLANTYNE

Squint to see the shadow value pattern; use your micro nib for those areas. Wait for a few seconds for the pen line to set. Test a small area. Place a very light wash over all value areas, reserving lightest areas—highlights in particular—as blank paper, building up washes gradually, as you did before.

EVALUATE

Evaluate as you would for any value drawing, from a distance, once your wash has set. Ask yourself if any areas need some darker wash. You can put more pen work over areas to deepen values, adding more contrast. You can also put washes over the pen work—but never use pen on a wet surface.

These drawings demonstrate the effectiveness of subtle gray washes. Let light layers of wash dry between applications if you want to achieve darker values slowly, with greater control. STUDENT DRAWINGS, FROM TOP, BY SANDY FITZMAURICE (SMALLER BRUSH), JIM HOHORST (TAPE ROLL), AND A. GASTON (LARGER BRUSH)

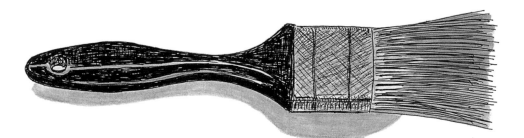

"When someone in class said she took two hours to do a drawing, I felt much better, because I always feel that I take too long."
—STUDENT KATHLEEN LEITAO

"I enjoyed layering the wash and getting it a little darker in some spots, and I was happy with the shading and the scale, even if I couldn't get all the lines the way I would have liked— but it still worked in the end." —STUDENT KIM NIGHTINGALE

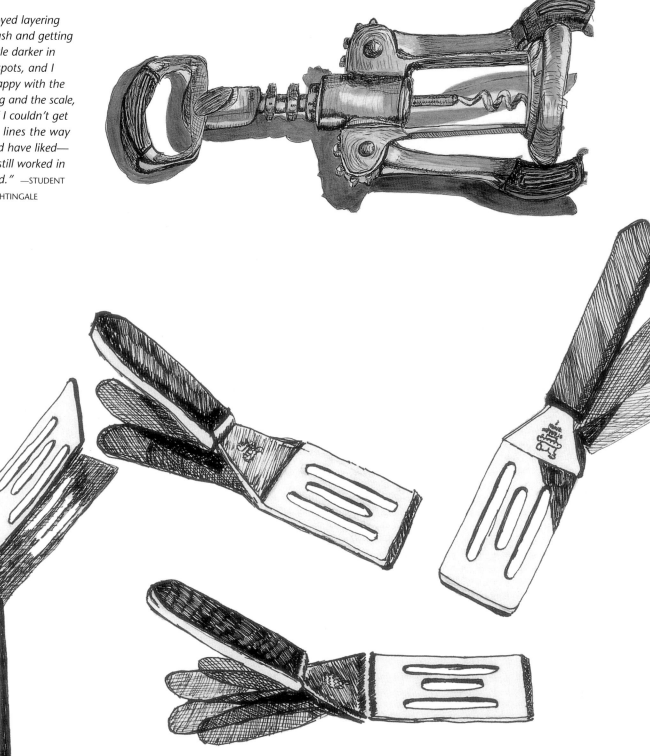

"If you have some nice lines, some nice shading, it can be pleasing even though it wasn't exactly what was on the table. It's a piece of art, not an exact replication. Don't beat yourself up so much!" —STUDENT ELLEN S. GORDON

Homework

Have fun with multiple possibilities. Play with techniques and materials. Now that you're familiar with wash, experiment with direct mixing and application of darker washes. Send someone a piece of "mail art"; use a postcard-size format, or if larger, apply a first-class stamp. Let a bunch of friends in on your activity by photocopying your drawings (use the black-and-white setting on a color laser printer to get a full range of grays), and send them out as mailing multiples— or scan and e-mail them.

"I hadn't taken a real art class since I was a kid. I was afraid to try, intimidated by all the details. So when we had the assignment to do the pen and wash, I wanted to do the cattails, but I was so worried about the wash and all those overlapping leaves and all those shadows to draw. I used a pencil sketch underdrawing for overall shape and placement, then just started at one end and worked my way to the other. No stopping or erasing. I realized it wasn't like this was going to be taken out and put on a public wall for critique. I could just start over if I wanted to, but I had to keep going until I finished. I was so happy when I saw that it was actually recognizable as cattails!" —STUDENT TRACEY M. ROBINSON

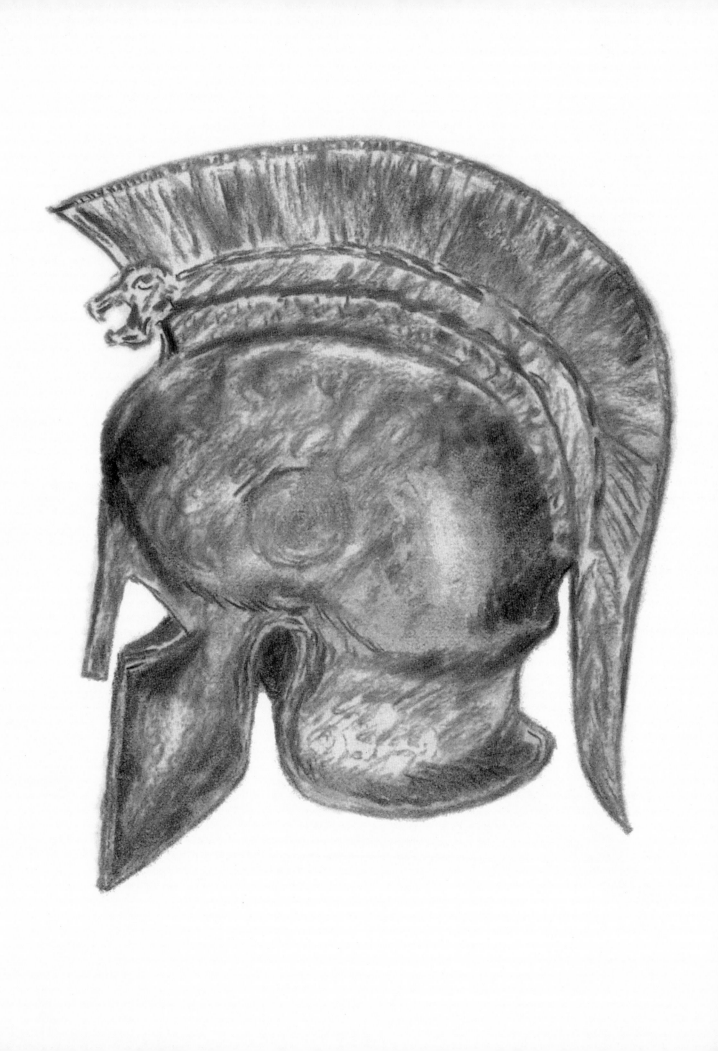

CHAPTER 6

Expanding Value Technique: Charcoal

"Grace, or the Tao, always surrounds us; whenever we are open for a moment, it enters into us."

—HERMANN HESSE

Many wonderful textures can be made with charcoal, as well as a wider range of values offered by the velvety-rich blacks it can produce. Beginners usually enjoy the opportunity to press the charcoal into paper and use their fingertips to blend. See what you think.

Leaning on your charcoal drawing can damage it. To prevent that, place a sheet of paper over parts of the drawing you're not working on, so your arm can rest there as you work on another area.

You'll be working with vine charcoal, a twiglike form of the medium that is often called "forgiving," because it erases so well (as opposed to compressed charcoal or charcoal pencils, which do not). Although you draw with its point, you'll use it most often by rubbing a small portion lengthwise on your paper to create a ribbon of gray. Pressure and release of pressure on paper creates varying values, as does adding layers, smudging, and erasing to lift off layers.

Vine charcoal is very responsive to touch; using a finger-painting technique in the charcoal dust creates further expressive possibilities. By the same token, be careful not to brush against or lean across the drawing, because the surface will be affected. As for subject matter, go to the market and head straight for the produce section, where appetizing still-life subjects abound. But I warn you that shopping for suitable models there can attract attention. My personal fruit and vegetable "audition" includes testing nature's products to see if they can stand up unassisted. This requirement involves posing prospective models. Will they topple and roll onto the floor or stand proudly under the lights? Allegiance to your art may cause fellow shoppers to back away from you while you separate the winners from the runners-up.

SUPPLIES FOR THIS CHAPTER

5 sticks vine charcoal
newsprint pad
14"-×-17" drawing pad
kneaded eraser
writing-pencil eraser
paper towels
Q-Tips
gray or other middle-value cloth

"I really like charcoal. It was easy to rub off. You didn't have to go get the eraser and rub away. Just smudge it off and start again."

—STUDENT PUSHPA KAPUR

OPPOSITE:
DRAWING BY STUDENT
JOHN F. X. PELOSO

Nature's Best Models

ood starters for level-one subjects in this chapter are solid-colored fruit, particularly those with uniformly light skins, such as Bosc pears or Golden Delicious apples. Scarred fruit is fine. It can give character to your subject—like a dueling scar!

Level-two subjects are more challenging: eggplant, lemons, colored peppers, Hubbard and acorn squashes, pumpkin, Red Delicious apples, multicolored apples, peaches, and pears. Treat yourself to a selection (you can always eat what you don't draw). Some artists can't resist a beautiful green cabbage with large, billowing leaves. As daunting as they are, cabbages do tempt beginners, who often get wonderful results. But as

a general rule, avoid very complex subjects like pineapple (too much detail) and oranges (the pitted skin is the only distinguishing feature, which is difficult to draw).

As you unpack your fruit and veggies at home, put them in a value scale for practice. Then you'll be set to start your charcoal sampler.

"I liked working in pencil, but I didn't like it as much as drawing in charcoal. I can't get the drama out of my pencil that I can out of the charcoal."
—STUDENT JAMIE KEEVER

EXERCISE: CHARCOAL SAMPLER

Let's get a feel for vine charcoal and your kneaded eraser, finger blending, and/or Q-Tip blending—your choice. Use your newsprint pad for this one, and spread your work over as many pages as you'd like. When you've completed these exercises, take a fifteen-minute break and study them at a distance so you can appreciate the texture and dimensional quality inherent to the charcoal medium.

1 Snap off a 1-$1/2$" piece of charcoal. Holding it between your thumb and first two fingers and rub its side on paper until you get a smooth path of gray.

2 Play with the charcoal, looping, scribbling, and making any marks that occur to you. Smooth areas with your finger; experiment with erasers.

3 Make a long, serpentine, ribbon-candy mark by alternately pressing down and letting up pressure as you move the charcoal down the page, pulling from side to side.

4 Create two value scales. For the first, press down and rub back and forth to make a very dark square. Continue to rub while pulling away from the square, letting pressure decrease, leaving a

gradually lighter trail. For the second value scale, fill in five squares of different values. Smooth each with your finger and reapply charcoal to adjust values.

5 Push down hard to see just how dark you can make your charcoal. If pressure gives you only reluctant, pale marks, you may have a faulty stick; sometimes there's a bad stick in the pack of soft vine charcoal, so try another piece to get deep, blackish grays.

6 Make two marks very close to each other. Use your finger to blend one area into the other.

7 To create a crisp edge, move your grip to one end of your charcoal, then press down while pulling it over the paper toward you. Move your grip to the middle of the stick and do the same, with no pressure on either end, to create a softer edge.

KNEADED-ERASER TECHNIQUES

Think of your kneaded eraser as a brush full of white paint. You can create numerous effects by erasing through a layer of charcoal to reveal white paper, in any shape you desire. You'll be able to blend and soften shapes with it, create small highlights, trim the edge of an object by erasing around it, and intensify light areas.

Use your kneaded eraser until it gets too much charcoal buildup on part of it. Then, simply fold that darkened area back into the eraser and knead a bit to uncover a clean surface. Although the eraser on an ordinary writing pencil is also a useful tool when working with charcoal—especially for getting into tiny, hard-to-reach areas—it's not the renewable resource the kneaded eraser is. But both kinds of erasers are effective for feathering edges and defining crisp ones.

8 Make three 2" squares of a dark, middle-gray value. Smooth the surfaces.

9 Pinch up a small nub of *clean* kneaded eraser, without pulling it from the whole eraser. Use this eraser tool to create a small, light area in the midst of the first dark-gray square you prepared earlier. Push down on the eraser and wiggle, rather than wipe, to make the desired shape. Repeat if you want a lighter mark. This is a great technique for bright, crisp highlights.

10 Use your eraser tool to soften an edge of your small, light area. Use delicate strokes to break down the crisp edge. Break down one side of your square this way as well.

11 Make your second square a bit smaller by erasing a column of charcoal from three sides. Maintain a firm pressure while you drag the eraser in the appropriate direction. You might have to scrub a little to get the surface thoroughly erased. You can create a curvy edge this way as well. Try it on the fourth side.

12 Bear down firmly and drag the eraser diagonally to make a triangle out of the third square.

13 With the point of your charcoal, draw contour lines, some dark, some light. Soften them with your eraser tool. Use this technique when an outline is too prominent.

14 Make a gray value square. Wipe it with the flat side of your eraser to subdue texture.

15 Outline an irregular shape, then fill it in with some subtle, multidirectional, flowing strokes that echo the shape. Smooth an area.

16 Repeat #13. Tame those active strokes with horizontal grounding strokes parallel to the bottom of your page, to reinforce level ground. This is a a good way to tame overactive cast shadows.

Shadow Sketches

P ut some of your fruits and veggies on a plain, middle-value surface. A plain gray cloth (or other middle-value color) is ideal. Light them to bring out dimensionality. Using your 14"-×-17" drawing pad, make a few sketches in charcoal, concentrating on contour and those shadow shapes you identified in Chapter 4, just to get a feel for the medium. Practice smudging the charcoal dust with your finger, or if you'd prefer, substitute a Q-Tip for a similar effect.

"I discovered a medium that I loved, charcoal, where I could be messy, spontaneous, and less precise."

—STUDENT SHERRY ARTEMENKO

The contrasting dark values of skillfully applied cast shadows anchor items to the surface they sit on and enhance a drawing's overall visual appeal as shown on these two pages. STUDENT DRAWINGS, BY SHERRY ARTEMENKO (PEAR, TOP) AND PAMELA M. HEBERTON (PEPPERS, BOTTOM)

"I came to drawing class with the idea of painting—eventually. I found I loved the way charcoal went on in layers. It reminded me of painting."

—STUDENT JANE WOLANSKY

STUDENT DRAWINGS, BY MARY JO FUSARO (PEACHES, TOP) AND SHERRY ARTEMENKO (LEMONS, BOTTOM)

Step-by-Step Charcoal Study

Find your "beloved" again—a subject you are attracted to and willing to spend time with. Adjust its position and lighting, if necessary. Turn off other lights and close curtains/blinds to create more dramatic lighting. Observe the objects in your setup and squint to block out detail. You want to see two basic, interlocked dark- and light-value shapes on each object. Where dark meets light, the transition is soft, blended. It bears repeating: It's crucial to squint to see those shadows more clearly.

"As the only man in class, I was surprised that several classmates were stylistically far more bold and assertive than I, using much sharper value contrasts, for example. (So much for gender stereotypes!)"
—STUDENT GEORGE STEVENS

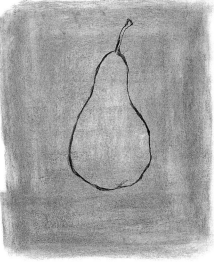

STEP 1: CREATING A GROUND.
A ground is an overall background gray. It will supply you with a middle value against which you can better judge the other grays. Cover your paper with the same value as your table surface, applying charcoal in vertical and horizontal strokes, or in a flowing manner, if you prefer. (You don't need to use the entire page; a border of white paper may remain.) Keep strokes close enough together to avoid a striped effect. Rub them down with a paper towel to get a soft, overall gray with a suedelike finish.

STEP 2: DRAWING THE SUBJECT.
With the point of your charcoal, make a slow, careful contour drawing of your subject. Include any edge, outside or inside (such as the grooves of a pumpkin) that can be turned into a contour line. *Put specific character into your drawing by recording what you see, not a generalization.* What you think is round may actually be somewhat bumpy, often angular. Slow down to get that in there. Note that stems have two sides, like miniature tubes. If there's some part that's particularly hard to draw, practice it with pen or pencil on scrap paper. If you don't like your contour drawing, wipe it out, lay in more ground, then smooth it over with a paper towel. Are you sure you want this subject? You can change your mind!

STEP 3: DETERMINING RELATIVE VALUE. To determine the basic value relationship between ground and subject, squint until your eyes are almost closed. Relative to the surface it sits on, is your subject darker, lighter, the same value, or a mix of both? See "Strategies for Creating Shadows and Dimension" (page 98) for tips on how to assess and adjust those relationships, which are really important if you want to create the illusion of dimension on your paper. This pear was both the same as, and darker than, the ground. First, I fingerpainted the inside of the pear to make its texture different from the ground. Then I rubbed in those values around the pear that I noticed made its contour stand out.

STEP 4: APPLYING SHADOW VALUES. Squint to see the object's shadow shape. Fill that in, leaving the transition edge soft. Fill in the cast shadow and erase to create light values within the shadow on the object. Keep the latter darker than values in the light area. Create textures and highlights—if they're present—by lifting out charcoal dust with an eraser where needed. Blend and soften with Q-Tips or fingers. Continue to record value shapes within larger value areas. Use your charcoal and eraser technique to reach the degree of finish you like.

STRATEGIES FOR CREATING SHADOWS AND DIMENSION

Establish the overall value of an object first, then always make shadows darker than the object. Shadow values are relative to the objects they lie on. For example, the shadow on a lemon is lighter than the shadow on an eggplant.

The texture of an object must be differentiated from the ground; otherwise, the object will look flat and transparent. Here are four different ways to adjust the value relationship between ground and subject to create the illusion of dimension on your paper:

IF YOUR SUBJECT IS DARKER THAN THE GROUND: Fill in its overall middle value until it's darker than the surface it sits on.

IF YOUR SUBJECT IS LIGHTER ON ONE SIDE, DARKER ON THE OTHER: Apply a basic overall value, then work to differentiate values on either side.

IF YOUR SUBJECT AND GROUND ARE THE SAME VALUE: Change the texture inside your subject by rubbing charcoal around until its texture differs from the surface it's on.

IF YOUR SUBJECT IS LIGHTER THAN THE GROUND: Rub it with your finger or an eraser to remove some charcoal until the subject is lighter than the surface.

The addition of skillfully placed highlights and charcoal values to careful contour drawings creates the illusion of dimension in these studies. STUDENT DRAWINGS BY, FROM TOP CLOCKWISE, DIANE M. H. SCHULTZ (PEAR), KATHLEEN LEITAO (SQUASH), SUSAN DILORETO (SQUASH), AND ANNE BALLANTYNE (LEMON, APPLE)

When you apply values, move the side of your charcoal along with the shape of the object, as illustrated so well in this example. The movement is like a cross-country skier flowing over a landscape of hills and valleys, always following their changing contours. DRAWING BY STUDENT MARY JO FUSARO

More Complex Subjects

Level-two choices from your veggie collection are somewhat more complex. However, proceed using the same methods. The following helpful hints are for approaching particular subjects:

- *Count out the number of segments in lobed subject matter, such as pumpkins, acorn squash, or colored peppers. On a pepper each highlight shape is specific in shape to the surface it sits on. Keep your eraser clean. There's a real payoff to careful rendering of these.*

- *Eggplants have varying darks, not just one. Some highlights are crisp, others can be swabbed with the side of eraser. Don't forget to draw the stem end carefully, observing that it has a variety of values.*

- *Cabbages require an overall value against which one can pick out ribs with an eraser. To appear round, its entire surface, including patterns, is affected by shadow values.*

- *Lemons require a light layer of values against which little pores can be picked out with an eraser. The overall shape is what says* lemon, *not tons of surface detail.*

WHEN IS A DRAWING FINISHED?
The more you observe and add to your drawing in the way of value detail, the more closely you replicate the dimensionality in front of you. But some artists make charcoal studies rapidly, in a more direct fashion. Fast finishers in class will glance around, wondering if they should keep going, even though they feel finished with their drawing. If that sounds like your experience, examine your work at a distance to help you decide. If you like it, it's complete. The *drawing* rules, more than the initial aim or directions. If you aren't satisfied, follow the evaluation procedure, until you are. Sometimes a nice drawing pops out quickly. If it does, accept the gift!

Now, take a break and take a look. Position your paper so you see both drawing and subject at once, from the same vantage point from which you drew. Find three aspects of your drawing that you can improve. Take a fifteen-minute break before doing more.

Improving Your Charcoal Drawing

To refine your value shapes, observe how those shapes fit together, just as you did in Chapter 1. Note how some shapes have crisp edges, others soft. Use your sampler tools to feather the edges to soften them or use your finger to blend. You'll bear down on one side of the charcoal for crisp ones, or use your eraser to soften an edge in the co-joined negative space.

Highlights are value shapes as well, with crisp and soft edges. Sharp edges have precise downward dabbing; soft ones call for pulling at the highlight edge to break it down and blend it slightly into the surrounding darker value. To make the highlight stand out, you need contrast with a surrounding darker value. Make sure you have enough contrast by putting the surrounding value on first, overlapping the planned highlight area. Then use a clean eraser tool to dab and lift out charcoal to reveal the paper white.

REFINING YOUR CONTOUR LINE

Initially, you'll rely on your contour line to represent your subject. However, we see both soft or crisp edges due to contrast in value shapes, not because there's an actual line around objects. Contour lines are an artistic device; they don't correspond directly to how we see the world. Look around you. Find two objects with contrasting values slightly overlapping. Do you see the edge because of an actual outline? Or is it the contrast between two different value shapes that you see?

If needed, soften your contour line by running a Q-Tip, eraser tool, or finger over it. Reinforce the edge here and there with contour line. Do what works to make your drawing interesting and satisfying. This is your choice, because it's art, not reality.

IMPROVING DIMENSION

When you want to create the illusion of dimension, the same principles apply for all value drawings. Spotting problems and the solutions for them, as presented in Chapter 4, can be applied to charcoal as well. To review:

- *If a three-dimensional object looks flat, its contours are too uniformly emphasized or three values aren't present.*
- *If an object looks fragmented, it lacks middle values and/or has overly sharp transitions between values.*
- *If an object is vague and seems to fade, it lacks value contrasts and clear edges.*

NEW SOLUTIONS

The use of your kneaded eraser with charcoal allows you to extend values into the lighter, brighter range, just as you did with darker values in pencil and wash. It's not that you can go lighter than the white paper provides. However, by using the eraser effectively, you can create the impression of a more dramatic value range.

If your still life has high contrast but you haven't captured the effect to your satisfaction, perhaps you need to push the light areas further—especially if you've pushed the darks as far as seems accurate. This most often occurs in a large, light area, rather than a small highlight. While keeping an eye on the still-life contrast, gradually scrub the lightest areas with your eraser. Try to match the extent of high contrast as you erase. Remember, you can add charcoal back if you take it too far.

You may not feel comfortable with this technique now. When you do try it, work a small area. Evaluate its effect from a distance to see if it helps. This can be done in small, controlled steps.

"I had three different colored peppers, so I got those out. I put the outline in first, to see where they were in space, then the local values. For lighter areas, I picked up layers of charcoal, mostly with my finger. The yellow pepper was hardest." —STUDENT STEPHANIE SEIDEL

"What I loved about this drawing was how physical it was working with the charcoal. Rubbing and redrawing, using the eraser to pick up a bit here and there. My whole body could get involved when I put in the ground. I could dance it!" —STUDENT PATRICIA R. SPOOR

Additional Tools

"In looking at everybody's work, one thing I noticed is the amazing power of the little white shape, the little white rectangle or white line." —STUDENT JANE WOLANSKY

Tortillons, stumps, and charcoal pencils are adjuncts to vine charcoal and kneaded eraser. Tortillons and stumps are pointed cardboard cylinders that come in a variety of diameters, to be used for fine blending. Charcoal pencils come in various hardnesses, as do carbon pencils. But they don't produce that lovely, grainy swathe of gray you create with the side of vine charcoal. However, you can draw with the point, and also fill in pencil style with them.

PROTECTING YOUR CHARCOAL DRAWING

Charcoal is the most fragile drawing medium. If you brush against it accidentally, your work can disappear. For this reason, charcoal drawings should be sealed with fixative, but it must be handled with extreme care, because the fumes are toxic. Follow the cautionary instructions on the fixative can. *Spray outdoors if possible. Indoor spraying should be only in a well-ventilated area that you can then leave. Never spray inside your living space.*

Overly active cast shadows (above, left) can be tamed with level strokes (above, right) that mimic the horizontal direction of the table surface.

Homework

Once you finish your first piece on charcoal ground, forget the ground and draw directly with your charcoal point. Fill in values and shadows to the extent you want. Experiment and enjoy yourself. Extend your choice of subject matter, but stay with multidimensional objects. Make sure to light them for more dramatic effects.

"I signed up for a five-hour workshop. As the day unfolded, I followed each step of instruction, each little success giving me the courage to continue. When I first looked at the array of fruit and vegetables, the cabbage seemed to wink at me. I thought, No you don't—I'll do an apple. Then I thought, What the hell? What's the worst that can happen? It won't turn out, and I'll try something else. As the cabbage began to take shape on my paper, it was working. I just followed the lines, drew what I saw, erased the charcoal to show the light. I relaxed, didn't worry, had fun. I nearly cried several times during the day—not from fear, but from the joy of knowing that this part of me was being accessed. I could actually learn how to draw!" —STUDENT NANCY OPGAARD*

Drawing the Face, Frontal View

"When Gertrude Stein saw my canvas, she protested,
'It doesn't look like me!' I told her, 'You'll see.
One day you'll end up looking just like your portrait.'"

—PABLO PICASSO

Luckily for anyone who wants to draw it, the relationships between the features of the face and the rest of the head are set in bone. These relationships are surface manifestations of the underlying skull structure, something which, except for the mobility of neck and jaws, is a rigid structure. This is good news for the beginner artist, since there are fewer variables to deal with. The real challenge in drawing the face is perceptual, rather than technical. It can be a struggle to accept what is seen instead of what is stored as a symbol in the mind. Most beginners are still at the symbol stage when it comes to faces, a place useful for practical, as opposed to aesthetic, functioning.

The biggest challenge in drawing the face is
observing it in a fresh, new way, seeing what's there
as you never have seen it before.

What do I mean by "symbols"? Picture the lollipop head on the stick neck. Large, staring eyes rimmed with spike lashes. The nose with ball-bearing nostrils. Hairstyle worn simply but efficiently on the tip-top of the head. It works. It says *face*. But is it art? Are those symbols based on actual knowledge of the human face? We know our own face and the faces of close friends and family—but long ago, we stopped paying attention to specifics.

We've learned to see largely for survival purposes, so we have moved our seeing functions into general categories, those recognitions that will allow us to have our needs met. We know noses, but darn if we have ever really observed one as carefully as when our grandfather bounced us on his knee. So when we say we can't draw a nose, we're saying we know one when we see one, but haven't really taken the time to observe how all those pieces hook up. Who knows one's own nose? It's time to take a look.

The following pages will show you what to look for, as well as the best and easiest way to draw it. Remember, if you haven't been to this destination before, you aren't supposed to know how to get there!

SUPPLIES FOR
THIS CHAPTER
2H and 2B pencils
14"-x-17" drawing pad
scrap paper
Pink Pearl eraser and
    writing-pencil eraser

"When I draw, it
takes me a long,
long time. I know
I'll never get
anyone else to sit
still long enough—
so I draw myself."

—STUDENT JIM
HOHORST

OPPOSITE:

DRAWING BY STUDENT

SHERRY ARTEMENKO

Studying the Face: Start with Your Own

Use your own face at first, since with this subject matter, you're the one most likely to be generous with your time. Find a mirror that allows you to see your whole face. Light it from one side to give yourself some clear value contrast. Make sure you don't create a complicated set of shadows.

But first, let's deal with some typical responses to using yourself as a model: "My nose is too big." "*My* nose is too short." "I hate my hair." "I have too many wrinkles." If any of such imagined, or even true, concerns are about to stall you, don't let that happen. Using yourself as a model is absolutely the best, and almost the only, way you're going to learn how to draw the face. And frontally is the way to start. Although we have a frontal view of faces less frequently than a three-quarter view, which encompasses everything slightly turned away from frontal to nearly profile, both eyes are not fully seen in three-quarters, whereas the frontal view allows us to see all features clearly.

We're going to use a general structure that can be applied to all faces, regardless of age, gender, or ethnicity. It will provide you with flexible guidelines to be modified according to the particulars of the model you use. Your observations take priority over the guidelines. When you realize something is really "off" in your drawing, return to the basic rules of proportion to help you. You'll learn to draw the frontal view of the face using exercises that fall into four groups:

- *Blocking in basic facial proportions*
- *Developing individual features*
- *Shaping the face*
- *Creating dimension by adding values*

Students often begin by saying these exercises are too hard, but by the time they've completed their first face drawing, they have found the process fascinating. There's a lot of information to take in, but unlike in the classroom, at home you can take as much time as you'd like to read, observe, and apply what you learn in stages. Don't aim for perfection. Your aim is to take in the written and visual material, and continue to build on it through practice and ongoing observation.

EXERCISE: BLOCKING IN

As you begin this first step, placing features, it's instructive to check these proportions while observing your own face, without drawing at all until you're ready. Read through and then refer to the illustration. You'll build the next step on top of this first exercise, so make sure your lines are light and erasable as you sketch.

1 **An oval** (not a circle) represents the head. Make your oval about 10" high. You'll use this shape as a foundation, modified later. Keep your oval lines soft, searching, nothing rigid or dark.

This "symbol" character lurks in all of us. The sure way to replace this image is by observing and recording new information about the face.

Practice your ovals on scrap paper until you feel comfortable.

2 Draw **horizontal lines** at the top and bottom of the oval, to establish the top of the head and the chin level.

3 To find **eye level,** sketch a horizontal line halfway down the oval. Eye level is a horizontal line right through the center of the pupil, when the eyes are looking straight ahead.

4 To find **midline of the face,** sketch a vertical line from top of head to chin level, at right angles to eye level, dividing the face into two matched sides. We don't see this line, but it exists in the skull. Eye level, middle of front teeth, base of the nose, and middle of the chin are all on this midline.

5 To find **base of the nose-level line,** draw a horizontal line on the midline halfway between the lines for eye level and chin level. This represents the base, not the tip, of the nose. The tip is fleshy and in some of us dips down below the nose-level line.

6 To find middle of the **lips,** make a mark a third of the way down between the level lines for nose and chin. The lip mark is variable, but in general, lips are closer to the base of the nose than to the chin. As usual, you need to observe and be true to the specifics of your model's face. To establish mouth width, sketch two droplines from the middle of eye ovals two and four. Extend the mouth mark horizontally to meet them.

7 To establish **eyeballs,** draw five horizontal ovals along the eye-level line, bisected by it, so the line goes through all five, like a string through beads. Compare and adjust the sizes of your ovals to make them all equal in size and shape. Maintain a light and generalized line. Avoid "Orphan Annie" circles. You're representing the whole eyeball

at this stage, not just the part visible between the lids, and not just a symbol.

8 To establish **nose length,** draw a triangle with its apex at a point on eye level centered in the middle eye oval. Place its base at the nose-level line.

9 To establish **nose width,** drop a plumbline from the inside corner of the second and fourth ovals to nose level. The space between these lines at nose level equals the width of the bottom of the nose. Bottom of the nose, triangle base, and the horizontal length of the central eye will all be about the same.

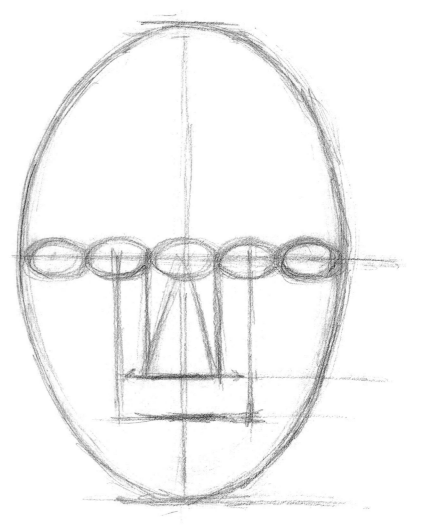

This "jack-o'-lantern" image gives you the foundation upon which you'll develop the face. The relationships formed around the triangle are the core proportions of the human head. They'll go a long way to help you overcome the common perceptual pitfalls in drawing the face.

AVOID

Be careful not to make:
- Circle for the head
- Circles for eyes
- Midline not vertical
- Eye level not horizontal
- Nose level too high
- Eye level too high
- Eye ovals on top of eye level
- Blocking in lines dark, unbroken

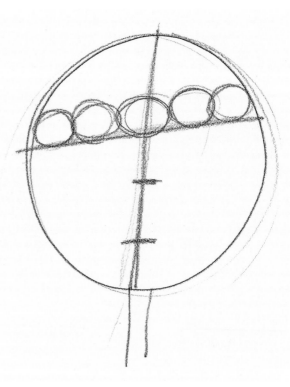

CONSTRUCTIVE EVALUATION

Before going to the next step, put your picture on the wall and view it from a distance to make sure that:

- *Eye level is halfway down the oval, parallel to bottom of page, with midline parallel to side of paper.*
- *Eye-level line goes through the ovals, not under them.*
- *Nose level is halfway between eye and chin levels.*
- *Mouth level is one-third distance (not one-half) between nose and chin.*

EXERCISE: DEVELOPING INDIVIDUAL FEATURES

This exercise starts to build individual features. Refer now to your own face and to the illustration for guidance. The following pages contain more detailed instructions for developing each feature. Use light, directional lines to:

1 Establish the **bridge of the nose,** bisecting the eye-level line.

2 Draw **eyes,** building lids within the eye oval, on the oval, covering part of the iris.

3 Place **brows,** duplicating the space shape between crease and brow.

4 Draw the **mouth** with the centerline broken and darker than the outline.

5 Structure the **nose** in parts. Note the angle of nostrils and leave space between them.

6 Verify the **vertical lineup** of mouth corners with the pupils, and sides of the nose with tear ducts.

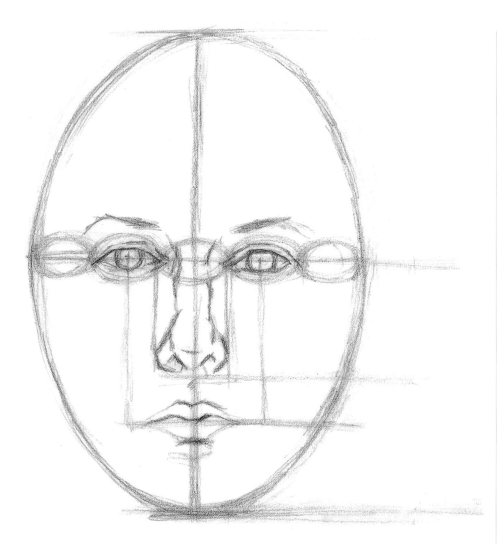

Use this example as general reference only for developing individual features. Of course, when drawing your own face or any other, copy only those unique features, not the ones shown here. Drawing in features is a bit like arranging a still-life of small objects. You focus on each interesting cluster of value shapes and contours, then take in their relationships to a larger symmetrical structure.

AVOID

Be careful not to make:
- Oval too wide
- Eyes too large, irises too big
- Sides of nose attached to tear ducts
- Nose too short, bottom too small
- Mouth too high

- Oval too long
- Eyes too small for oval
- Nose too long
- Mouth stretched

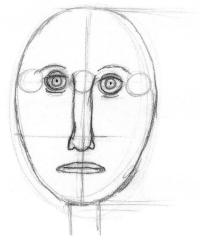

BEING YOUR OWN MODEL

After you've blocked in the general relationships among the features, start referring specifically to your own face. Begin to sketch your own features on top of the blocked-in oval you've prepared. Erase blocking-in lines a bit if they're dark, or they'll distract you when you draw. At first, it's difficult to be detached about your own face. It can be a strange new experience scrutinizing this person (you!) staring back at you. But self-study is an excellent aid in learning to draw the face.

To try drawing your own face, begin the same way, by blocking in proportions. Then focus on each individual feature, reporting on what you observe as accurately as you can. Look at your entire face as you work, to relate each feature accurately to the whole. And now that you've made a symmetrical basis for your face, it's time to tell the truth! The end of the nose is often wider than your markings; eye and eyebrow pairs often appear mismatched; and the eyes are sometimes not quite at right angles to the midline. However, the symmetrical guidelines will serve as a basis for comparison, enabling you to catch those particulars of your face. Sighting to line up features on the vertical is your best tool in evaluating specific placement of features.

EMOTIONAL EXPRESSION

Our faces are capable of expressing a wide range of emotions. We're aware that intense communication can issue from the eyes and is expressed at the corners of the mouth. However, the brow, cheek, nose, and jaws all have a part to play in our expressive capacity. To get an idea how the action of facial muscles creates your expression, watch yourself in the mirror as you make the face that corresponds to each feeling listed below. Ham it up to get full benefit as you say:

- *I couldn't be more surprised!*
- *Ick! This tastes awful!*
- *That was a wonderful experience!*

Repeat the exercises while your eyes are closed, with your fingers on chin, cheek, and brow, to make the experience even more revealing. Could you feel your facial muscles move up and down with your emotions? Although we're going to study the face in a composed state (at least you'll attempt to remain composed), it's helpful to become more sensitive to the expressive role of brow area, movement of the jaw, and even tension around the nose.

FINDING CENTER

The bridge of the nose marks the middle of the head, and is an anchor point for all facial features. Continue to use light sketching lines as you draw in the bridge. Yours may be somewhat triangular in shape or it may be columnlike. The bridge sits inside the central eye oval and is never wider than the bottom width of the nose.

If you wear glasses while you work, treat them as just another shape. Try to create lighting without direct highlight on the lens surface. DRAWING BY STUDENT STEPHANIE SEIDEL

EYES

Sketch the triangular shapes of your tear ducts pointing in at the nose within ovals two and four. That detail not only helps to shape your eyes, it establishes space needed for the orbital setting of the eyes. Look carefully at the steep angle of the contour of your upper lid that leads up from the tear duct and continues above the iris. This angle is significant to eye shape, and is often surprising to beginners, who assume it has a rounded shape.

Be careful not to make the eyes too large for the face, a natural tendency considering their importance to us emotionally. How can you avoid this common mistake? Be aware that the nose is longer than the lengthwise measurement of the eye. Compare the length of your own eye by sighting on the horizontal (end to end) and comparing it to the length of your nose on a vertical. This is the general proportion to maintain in your drawing. Check it against your drawing. If you have made the eye measurement longer than the nose, it's probably inaccurate.

The eyes are fraternal, not identical, twins. Look for the differences that make each one unique. You'll often see size and shape discrepancies, and sometimes, tilted eye levels that are not quite at right angles to the midline. Rely on contour drawing to capture the unique quality of each eye.

Still building on your initial blocking-in drawing, sketch in both upper and lower lids within ovals two and four. They'll be continuous to the contour of the tear ducts. Make sure upper lids overlap lower lids at the outside corner of each eye. The fleshy inner portion of the lower lid, not the lash line, rests against the eyeball. If a challenging area makes you darken and reinforce your lines, practice the feature on scrap paper to avoid doing that.

The crease of the eye, where the eyeball nestles into the bony orbit of the skull, usually mirrors the rise and fall of the upper lash line. Use the fleshy shape between the crease of the eyes and brow to help you sketch this area more accurately. Some eyes are hooded—that is, the crease of the upper lid isn't visible.

Sketch in the iris—the colored portion of the eye—as a slightly rounded cube. We often imagine we see the iris as a full circle, and mistakenly draw it that way. Usually, only when the eye is expressing extreme emotion or when it is very large, do we see the entire iris. Much of the upper rim of the iris is covered by the upper lid. The lower rim of the iris is often slightly overlapped by the lower lid.

Keep the pupil lighter than you think it is, to avoid the common tendency to make it too dark and more prominent than it is. The pupil will always be in the middle of the entire iris, but not in the middle of the iris that's showing.

BROWS

The brows angle up above the eye from the contour of the sides of the nose, then descend toward the temple. Avoid the "Arch Fiend" look that may occur if you let the brow continue to ascend. Feel the bony brow line that juts out over the eye where your eyebrows sit, to get a sense of the downward curve the brows will follow. Sketch in the brow as an angled shape, not as lots of hairs.

Use directional lines to build from an oval to an eye. Things to avoid (see below) are corrected here (left): Eyelids are reduced in size and placed inside original oval; entire iris does not show; tear ducts are now indicated; lashes to be added subtly, later.

AVOID

Be careful not to make:

- White of the eye too large
- Iris too large and fully visible
- Lids too large and outside original oval
- Spikey lash fringe

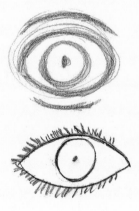

NOSE

Oh, no! The nose! Since you're apt to focus on eyes and mouths more often than on noses, take a really careful look at this feature before you start drawing. Sometimes beginners think the nose will look too prominent if they follow the blocking-in measurement; or what they see doesn't compute with what they think they should see. Many are reluctant to put what they see on paper for fear their observation is rude or wrong. For instance, a nose may have nostrils that don't match, perhaps because the nose tip turns slightly to one side. Draw it that way if that's what you see when achieving a likeness is important to you. Be true to what you see and it will move your skills ahead. Here are some basics to keep in mind.

If you've drawn the triangle, it will help you to assess nose size. The bottom of the nose is probably wider than you expected and often wider than the standard given, but rarely smaller, so make sure not to shrink it within the guidelines. It can line up with the inside rim of each iris. Lining up the sides of nostrils with the tear ducts is also helpful. The length of the nose, not including a wayward tip or two, is rarely longer than the guidelines, but is sometimes shorter. Modify the blocking-in measurements as needed to portray the nose you're drawing.

Think about the structure of the nose before drawing it. The long, upper surface is composed of a rigid shaft and a softer, more malleable, end. Together, they create the overall shape of the nose. The shaft has fewer value contrasts than the

The nose is successfully portrayed in this portrait with just a few delicate lines to suggest its complex shape.
DRAWING BY STUDENT
ANNE BALLANTYNE

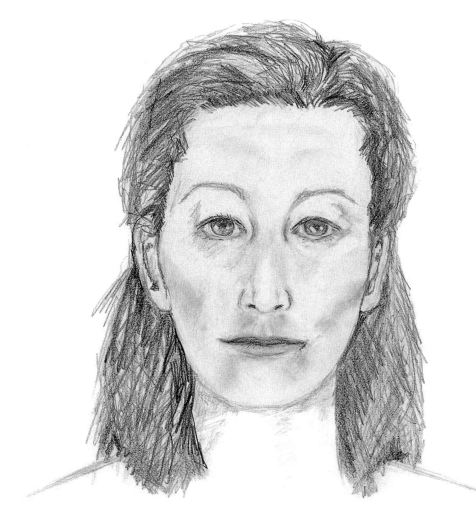

bridge and nostrils, so it's a less noticeable shape. Find the bump on your nose just below the bridge. Follow that shape until it narrows and transitions into the wider end of the nose. This basic structure appears thicker or thinner with each nose, just as the slope along the sides of the nose differs from one face to the next. Some faces have flatter noses with only subtle indications of this bony area, while it is angular and prominent in others.

The nose tip is rather like the end of a diving board, and springy as well. Pay special attention to the space between the nostrils at the very base of the nose, a key defining area. Due to its shared border with nostril openings, it has the greatest value contrasts. Capture the angle of this shared contour and you go a long way toward portraying the look of a specific nose. Check the angle in context with the entire face.

The fleshy contours of the nostrils share their contours with the upper surface of the nose, but sit on a lower plane. You may think of them as rounded, but look again. Many people have almost straight contours to the nostril, sometimes almost vertical or slightly angled in. Study the fleshy part that wraps around the nostril opening. Check it out on your own nose, but remember to level your head when you draw the nose.

EXERCISE: BLOCKING IN THE NOSE

Practice the complex structure of a nose on scrap paper first to reinforce your understanding of it before drawing the nose on your portrait. Then, working on the triangle you drew earlier:

1 Start at the **bridge** of the nose. Sketch in the changing movement of the **shaft** of the nose as it descends to the end, avoiding dark outlines. The side of the nose is a subtle area, best developed with values later.

Use light, directional lines to simplify shapes. Leave space between nostrils, and note that nostril coverings wrap around the openings.

2 Draw the **fleshy end** of the nose. This area often has a unique shape that can be defined by sketching its shared contours lightly. Document common borders with the adjoining fleshy nostrils and their inner angles.

3 Look for the middle dividing mark curving down from the end to the **base** of the nose. If the tip of the nose dips down over the blocked-in nose mark, the base of the nose won't be visible. The underside of the end of the nose will be defined by the values.

4 Sketch in **nostrils** with small, angular strokes, rather than making the classic "ball-bearing" symbols. Simplify the nostril covering contour with small directional lines, then check out angles within the whole face context. Avoid lining the upper curve of the nostrils with the base between them in one flowing line.

AVOID

Be sure not to draw a nose that looks at its end like (from top):
- The canary-beak nose
- The synchronized-swimmer's pinched nose
- The Miss Piggy nose
- The frilly-apron nose

115

MOUTH

Next, block in the mouth. The midline of the lips has an undulating movement that is more pronounced in some faces than others. The center of the upper lip may protrude slightly, producing a small overhang that fits into the center of the lower lip. I find lip contours comparable to a mountain-range elevation map. Does your mouth have high peaks and low valleys, gently rolling hills, or a fairly level surface?

Pay attention to the angle changes of the dark midline and upper-lip contour, which help greatly in capturing specific likeness to the model.

Both sides of the mouth generally line up on a vertical with the pupils, when eyes stare straight ahead. However, sides of the mouth don't always line up precisely, so don't stretch the lips to do so. A smaller mouth or a wider nose will mean the reference shifts slightly. Also notice that the lower lip is often more defined by the shadow just under it, than by a strong contour line leading to the corners of the mouth.

AVOID

Be careful not to draw:
- The lip outline as dark as the midline
- Rigid, unbroken, dark lines

TEETH

Avoid tangling with teeth as a beginner. Take a clue from the general absence of toothy smiles in the history of art, and keep your model's mouth shut. If you are determined to put the teeth in, remember the viewer sees only a few defined teeth at a time from one point of view. Treat them as an overall shape with minimized individual definition. Also note that when your mouth is closed, if your teeth are parted, dropping your lower jaw, your chin will lengthen, changing the original blocking-in proportion of the mouth to the rest of the face.

"Something clicked inside my mind and I was able to see things differently. Instead of looking at what I was drawing as a whole thing, I looked at its parts."

—STUDENT TRACEY M. ROBINSON

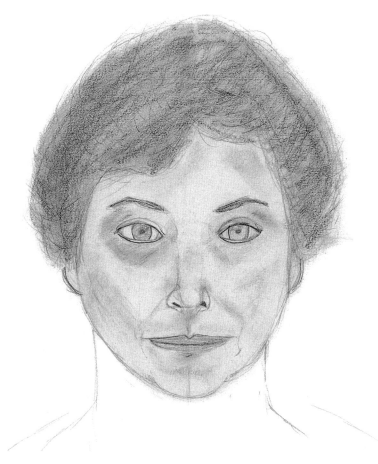

As each carefully observed featured is developed on the oval structure, a unique individual begins to emerge. Values and face shape specific to the subject are then added to create further likeness. DRAWING BY STUDENT AMY MILLER

EXERCISE: SHAPING THE FACE

Now that you have defined individual features, shaping the face is the next way to bring forth a likeness. Make a general observation of your face shape before you begin. Is your face squarish, rectangular, heart-shaped? Is it wider at the jaw than at the forehead, or just the opposite? Some people have a narrow, chiseled face. Others, a full one. The variety is endless, unique to each person.

1 Use long, angular **loose strokes,** holding your pencil farther away from the point than you did before.

2 Adjust the **contour of the face** relative to the features. Keep looking at your face to modify and verify your choices. Use a kind of artistic liposuction to remove unwanted or unecessary roundness as you reshape the original oval.

3 Adjust the **sides of the face,** which come closest to the features just above the brow line at the temples; below the cheekbones on a horizontal line with the bottom of the nose; and at the chin line on a diagonal down from the lower lip.

4 Now sketch in the **shape of the ears,** which extends from eyebrow level to the middle of the upper lip. (You'll define ears with values a little later, very lightly, to avoid drawing attention away from other features.)

5 Block in **hair as a shape,** like an interesting hat, and relate it to the developed face shape, rather than to the original oval. Use long, loose, angular strokes to suggest the hair's overall contour.

6 Further define the shape of the **forehead.** Record it as a puzzle shape that shares borders with the hairline and brows.

ABOVE: Use long, directional lines to define face shape. Pay attention to line angle relative to features as you work. Block in overall hair shape, not individual hairs.

LEFT: From left, is your face wider at the cheekbones, wider at the jaws, or rectangular in shape?

117

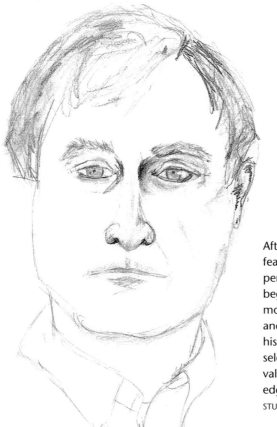

After developing features with light pencil strokes, this beginner has added more dimension and definition to his drawing with selective darker values and crisper edges. DRAWING BY STUDENT NANCY OPGAARD

With the addition of values in the eye, a sense of life and vitality begins to emerge in this portrait. DRAWING BY STUDENT PAMELA SHILLING

EXERCISE: CREATING DIMENSION BY ADDING VALUES

Now that features and face shape are defined on your original oval, begin to develop their dimensionality further by adding values. If you've retained a light, flexible line until now, you can build successfully on that. Use your 2B pencil until it's time to focus on skin values.

1 To turn a **blank stare of the eyes** into an expression with vitality, treat the varying value pieces of the iris as though they were part of an abstract puzzle. Within each iris there are light changes. Small, mosaiclike highlights are visible. Record these white shapes lightly, neatly merging their outlines with the surrounding iris value, which darkens as it nears the upper lids.

2 Avoid making the **pupils** an overly crisp, dark value, or you may create a Dracula-like stare. The pupil merges with the value in extremely dark eyes.

3 Treat the **recessed eye orbit** as a feature by drawing a shadow on either side of the nose and under the inside corner of each eye. These values lend depth to the face and keep the eye at an accurate distance from the nose. Sometimes artists think these shadows and so-called "bags" under the eyes add unflattering aging to a face, so they omit them. But even children's faces have some degree of both. The fullness under the eye corresponds to the lower half of the eyeball; the shadow, to the recessed orbit. The entire eye orbit from brow to under eye shadow can be filled in with a light shadow value.

4 We know **lashes and brows** are composed of individual hairs, but we see them as value shapes, with only some individual hairs visible. Fill in the value to the shape, then perhaps add a few characteristic hairs.

With features defined and face shape refined, adding values to your portrait contributes greatly to suggesting dimensionality.

Treat the iris carefully by adding values lightly. Fill in the local value precisely around the outline of highlight shapes. Add shadow values to the orbit area to give the face dimension.

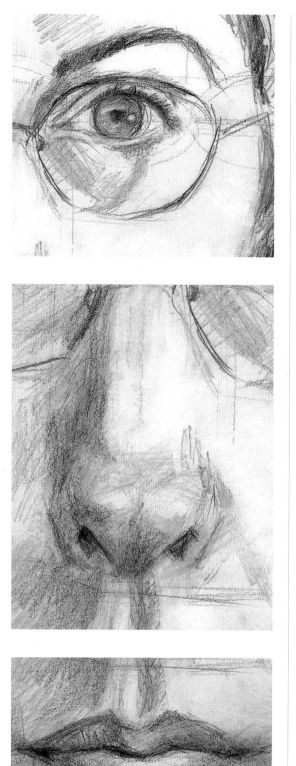

The end of the nose needs dimension to be convincing. Pay attention to value patterns, especially at the base of the nose, which will make the tip seem to push forward, as it actually does. Subtle shadow values along the shaft add dimension.

The darkest line of the mouth is the midline, not the outside contour. Value patterns there give fullness to the mouth. Shadow values under the lower lip and at the corners of the mouth add dimension.

5 Squint to find the value shapes along the **sides of the nose.** Accent values lightly on the side farthest from the light source. Place values under the tip, down and across the base to recess this area, making the tip of the nose seem to advance toward the viewer.

"The main thing I had to get over was trying to make myself look like what I want to look like instead of drawing exactly what I saw. I got past that by looking at the forms. My nose is just a shape, the way the handle of a cup is a shape."
—STUDENT SUSAN PARSONS

6 Fill in the overall value of the **mouth** before adding shadow values. The lower lip is usually fuller and lighter in value than the upper lip, because it catches more light. Give the midline of the mouth its darkest value, regardless of lipstick. Make that midline more like a long, slender value shape than a narrow line for a more expressive result. Notice how the sides of the mouth press into the flesh of the cheeks. Indicate this important area with two soft value shapes.

7 For **light skin tones,** switch to a 2H pencil, which shows less contrast to white paper, so it's easier to avoid the five-o'clock-shadow look where it isn't warranted. Then squint to isolate shadow shapes, and put light value in with a fine crayoning application. Light skin value doesn't need an overall value (though some beginners like the effect); white paper is accepted as local skin color.

8 For **darker skin tones,** use a 2B pencil. Fill in local value of darker skin tones partially, rather than completely—just enough to suggest overall skin value. To avoid flat cheeks, use soft, multidirectional strokes. Make shadow values darker than the basic skin tone. If skin values look too grainy, smooth with your finger and/or subdue with a 2H pencil.

9 Establish the overall local value of **hair** applied rapidly with long, crayoning strokes. Most beginners fill in with a gazillion hairs. If you do that, no overall hair color will emerge. Squint as you work over the first local value layer with smaller scribbles and more pressure. Darken hair at the crown near the roots, along the part line, behind the ears, and along the neck. With your pencil point, suggest straight, wavy, or curly hair with a few restrained strokes here and there, and add some loose tendrils that break the overall outline.

Sketch the overall shape of the hair. Then draw in its overall value. Then add deeper and lighter values, specific movement, and some individual hairs.

The hair should reflect the unique value range of the individual sitter. A dark overall value, specific texture references, and creation of dimension through shadow values all contribute to the success of this likeness. DRAWING BY STUDENT MIMI WEAKLEY

121

"I had never analyzed anyone's face with such scrutiny before. What power I held in my pencil—to create age or youth!" —STUDENT GAIL K. ROBINSON

10 For **blond, white, or gray hair,** fill in the overall middle gray that is under the lightest values. Erase back to create the lighter values. Use an eraser stroke that mimics the movement of the hair. Then add pencil lines over those areas to mimic the hair's movement—straight, wavy, or curly.

11 Add a **neck,** or you'll have a disembodied face (like Oz the Great and Powerful). Find the location on your chin where the sides of your neck become visible. Keep your contour light in this area or you'll detract attention from the face. Don't run the neck to the end off the page, or the eye will run with it. A slightly asymmetrical rendering generally looks better, so follow through slightly more on one side.

12 Suggest **shoulders** with a sloping triangular angle that begins toward the middle of the neck. A shirt collar would begin at this slope on the neck.

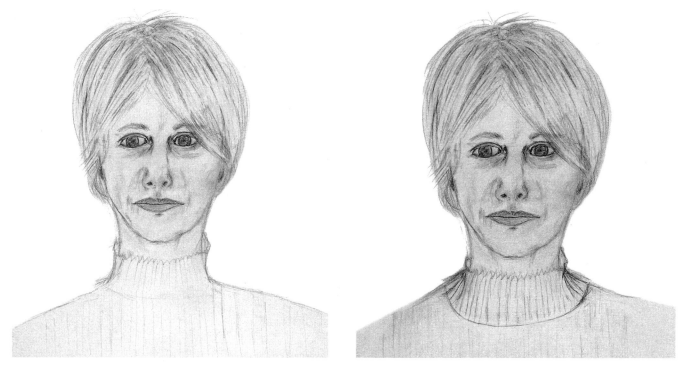

A good adjustment to the neck area, raising the shoulder slope, added accuracy to this portrait. DRAWINGS BY STUDENT KATHY EPSTEIN

Facial Expression

Facial expression is conveyed most dramatically by eyes and mouth. Aliveness is most apparent in the eyes. To portray expressive quality:

- *Fill in specific values carefully around highlights.*
- *Record the visible amount of iris and surrounding white of the eyes accurately.*
- *Consider the angle of each brow.*
- *Observe and record the midline of the lips carefully.*
- *Note the depth and angle of the crease between nose and mouth.*
- *Estimate the angle of the nostrils with care.*

If you're a careful reporter, you can simply let go into recording shapes, rather than try to figure out how to convey a specific mood at the outset. Specifics recorded will result in a specific mood. Remember, the "happy face" self-portrait is rare in art. What you're more likely to see is the artist's expression of deep concentration recorded as the self-portrait was created.

CONSTRUCTIVE EVALUATION

Place your self-portrait on a wall near a mirror, where you can see it and yourself at one glance. You may want to deepen or lighten some values on the eyes, hair, and brows. Emphasize shapes and darken values gradually. Make sure your overall mouth value is filled in, and you haven't left lips white.

Check expressiveness. Do your eyes look lively? If not, add highlight areas. Be sure their outlines are not darker than the surrounding value. If they are, fill in the iris value precisely around them. If your mouth has one rigid line, soften it with your eraser.

Rely on the shadow below the mouth to suggest the shape of the lower lip. Did you develop the indented value area of the cheek where it meets the sides of the mouth?

The face is your focus. If your eyes wander persistently to your hair or the nice earrings or necktie you might have added, erase and blur out those areas a bit. Be more selective in what you develop. Very active lines, high-contrast areas, and details draw the eye away from the features. Finally, if your neck, shoulders, and collar look like they were cut from steel, soften the angles.

ONGOING PRACTICE

Draw your face again in a couple of weeks. Or get someone else to pose for you. Have the model's gaze fixed on a spot near one of your ears, rather than looking directly in your eyes. If someone else is drawing with you, you can work simultaneously on portraits, alternating posing and drawing. Trade off after about four minutes per pose. Start with the bridge of the nose and one eye; switch, then draw the other eye; switch, and so on.

As with these beginners, if you've drawn the human face and recorded values and proportions accurately, then you're on your way; mark your progress with a big Hooray! STUDENT DRAWINGS BY ALEXANDRA TEBAY (LEFT) AND ANITA ST. MARIE (BELOW)

123

Facial Expression

RIGHT: *"The first time, it didn't look like a real person. As I went along, I'd get an eye right or part of the nose right. Finally, at number five, I got it to look like me."*
—STUDENT TRACEY M. ROBINSON

"At first, I was afraid of the self-portrait. But I ended up liking it, because it afforded me unlimited 'stare time.' We're conditioned to think staring is rude, particularly staring at individual facial features. The freedom to study a human face, to draw wrinkles and blemishes with abandon, came as a relief."

—STUDENT MARGARET ROSS

BELOW: *"I carried my self-portrait further than any of my other drawings. I was willing to redo. I did the eyes four times, the nose three times, the mouth twice."*
—STUDENT BARBARA KOPS

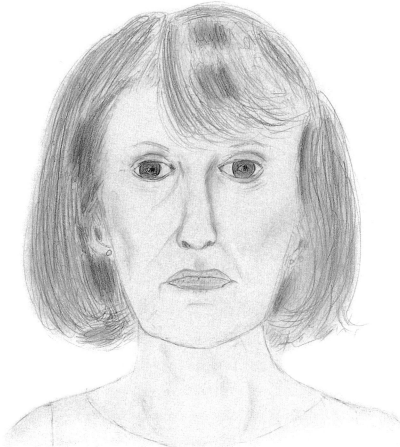

OPPOSITE: *"I turned out all the lights in the room and just used a single lightbulb, then set up a big mirror where I could sit and look at myself. I worked on my portrait three or four times. The first time, I did most of the drawing, over four or five hours. Then I put it on the mantle in my bedroom. I'd wake up and see the things that needed to be fixed. The nose didn't look right, and I'd go back and work on that with the mirror. The values changed a lot, but I started out very light. This was my first drawing course since seventh grade. I didn't expect to see it come out and look like someone I recognized—so I was pleased when other people knew it was me. There wasn't any conscious thought about the border. I have a lot of pent-up energy, and it needed someplace to go. As a self-portrait, it looked too calm without it."* —STUDENT JIM HOHORST

Homework

Look at people around you more carefully to continue developing your storehouse of information about the human face. Look in art books and photography magazines and annuals for frontal views of faces to draw.

As you learn to draw the human face, animal faces may become more interesting to you. You can more clearly relate to the extended-family concept when you notice similar features and structures in our face and the faces of dogs, cats, horses, and other "relative relatives" of ours. Notice, in particular, the expressive brow pads on your pets' faces.

Jim Honorss
NOVEMBER

CHAPTER 8

Drawing the Face, Profile View

"It seems to be a law of nature that no man is ever loath to sit for his portrait."

—SIR MAX BEERBOHM

ood news! You can use the same basic proportions for drawing the profile as you did for the frontal view of the face.

Beginning with an oval, features line up at right angles to the midline; eyes are placed halfway down the oval; nose base (not tip) is halfway between eye and chin; the midline of the mouth is about a third distance between the nose and chin. The major difference is that profile features are placed on either right or left side of the oval, depending on the pose you're drawing.

The profile is characterized by diagonals, rather than verticals and horizontals.

As usual, your energy will be stimulated by a good subject, so choose a face that appeals to you. You may have relatives and friends who would be happy to sit for their portrait–but you'll need a patient model. Otherwise, work with printed reference material. Use an easily discernible reproduction of a painting or drawing of a profile that has accurately rendered features.

Photographs of family members are rarely taken in true profile, and are often not crisp enough to be good sources, so you will probably have to turn elsewhere for reference material. Usually this means a trip to the art-history section of the library. If your library has photography magazines and annuals, they are also a good source to check. In choosing a good picture to copy, keep in mind that right-facing profiles work best for lefties, and the reverse for righties. When you photocopy a color picture, use the black-and-white setting on the laser copier to get an enlargement that reproduces gray tones accurately. While you're at the library, take the opportunity to photocopy at least a few profile portraits for further inspiration, after you've completed the exercises ahead.

SUPPLIES FOR
THIS CHAPTER
14"-x-17" drawing pad
2B and 2H pencils
Pink Pearl eraser or
 writing-pencil eraser

"The hair is still a problem for me— when I get back into drawing what I know is there, rather than drawing what I really see."

—STUDENT JANE
WOLANSKY

OPPOSITE: Based on a 1465 painting by Piero della Francesca. DRAWING BY STUDENT JANE WOLANSKY

127

Observing the Profile View

Your first step is to look at your model, and face up (yes!) to what you see, and significantly, what you don't see. For example, how much do you *actually* see of the profile eye? Actually, only one piece of the white, a slim disk for the iris, almost nothing of the pupil, and little, if anything, of the tear duct. The mouth can appear pretty minimal as well, in contrast to the frontal view.

What about the nose? Well, you can see a great deal, but only half of it. And what do you see in the center of the overall image of your profile source? Not much. Just the sideburn area in front of the ear.

Beginners tend to compensate for this "too little/too much" situation by making their own alterations. The ear begins to drift toward the nose; the eye enlarges; the mouth grows fuller; the nostril becomes smaller. Since beginning artists have a tendency to superimpose half the frontal face symbol onto the profile view, you'll need some help to keep your profile portrait true to the facts. Following the steps in the next exercises should do it.

EXERCISE: BLOCKING IN
Even though the profile is angular rather than rounded, a light oval is still a useful way to begin. Just as for the frontal view, for the profile, you'll use the same series of level lines to position the features in correct proportion to one another. Block in your profile features to left or right of the oval edge, depending on the direction your subject is facing.

1 Sketch an **eye-level** line halfway down the oval. Place the bridge of the nose on that line, slightly indented from the oval. Try to record the negative-space shape you see created by the indentation of the bridge.

Make your oval very pale, and keep your blocking-in lines sketchy and light. You'll be drawing over them as you develop individual features.

2 Sketch the **chin level** extended out beyond the oval. If your model's chin is tilted up or down, draw this line according to the tilt—but all horizontal lines should remain at right angles to it.
3 Sketch a **vertical line** from the bridge to the level line of the chin. This line represents the midline and also provides a safety net to keep you from recessing lip and chin features back too far and onto the oval.
4 Sketch level lines for **nose and lips.** Extend them onto the vertical midline. Both the skeletal base of the nose (not the tip) and the center teeth (under lips) are now marked on the midline where nose and chin-level lines meet it.

EXERCISE: DEVELOPING FEATURES
The relationship of facial features to one another in profile is the same as in the frontal view. The back contour of the

nostril still lines up on a vertical with the tear duct and the corner of the mouth with the front of the eyeball. But since details of tear ducts and pupils are difficult to see in profile, how can you draw correctly what you can't see clearly because of angle, distance, or shadows that make it impossible to find details? Line up general shape references for key features and explicit shapes if that is the extent of what you see. Accept the limits of what you can see, and your drawing will work. Don't make up details or move closer to your model to gather details, then apply them to a drawing done from a distance. The result will be an odd, unconvincing blend of near and far references. Instead, create an impression that duplicates your actual viewing experience. Draw value shapes with soft edges that produce an image with suggested, rather than specific, details.

1 Draw the **eyeball** as an oval bisected by the eye-level line. Leave space between it and the contour edge of the bridge.

2 Sketch diagonal lines on the oval to suggest **upper and lower lids.** Build lids over the eyeball, which is set back slightly underneath the lid overhang. Lids are like a protective awning that closes over the eyeball.

3 Draw the **iris** as a flat disk within the oval, with its top curve hidden by the upper lid; the pupil lies on the contour edge, closer to the upper lid, not in the middle of the visible portion. We see only a bit of the white of the eye. Avoid adding the iris on top of the eyeball, making the surface seem to protrude.

4 The **eyebrow** is generally formed by a sharp angle rising from close to the bridge, then a longer line that mirrors the angle of the crease or upper lid line. A value shape is more accurate than lots of hairs.

5 The distance from the back contour of the eye to back of the **ear** is the same as from eye level to chin level.

6 The contour line from **base of the nose** to upper lip may angle back or protrude forward. This contour begins under the nostril opening, not under the fleshy back of the nostril. Don't line it up on the midline, or you won't have left room to suggest upper teeth. Avoid giving the face a toothless look by paying careful attention here.

7 The **base of the lower lip** is on the vertical midline. Use your pencil as a plumbline to see which features lie to the right and left of this line. If your model faces left: The nose, mouth, and front of chin lie left of the line; eyes, brows, ears, rest of the chin, neck, and hair, line up primarily to the right; base of lower lip, bridge, and forehead line up nearest the midline.

Use directional lines to develop your profile drawing. Brow, lash, lip, chin, nose, and neck contours are all built with diagonal lines. All features placed on the oval break through it to some degree: The forehead angles back in toward the top of the head; the nose, along with the mouth and chin, protrude outward from the oval.

129

EVALUATION BEFORE ADDING VALUES

Look at your drawing from a distance to see if you have fallen into a "profile pitfall." If you kept your lines sketchy, you can still fix wandering features, then apply values and final touches. Here are possible "pitfalls" and how to recover from them:

Problem: Does the eye seem to bulge because you have put in more white than you actually saw there? *Solution:* Reduce white by bringing upper and lower lash lines closer together.

Problem: Is there too much iris or too dark a pupil? *Solution:* Place iris within oval and erase the intensity of the pupil.

Problem: Are the mouth and nose too far back onto the original oval? *Solution:* Line up key features along a vertical to ensure accuracy. Begin the upper–lip contour under the nostril opening, not at the back of it.

Problem: Do the lips look too full? *Solution:* In profile, the lower lip usually appears fuller than the upper. Both lips are built along diagonals. Make sure you haven't mixed in the frontal view here.

"This is the first formal art course I've ever taken. My prior experience was limited to drawing my favorite cartoon character in elementary school. Once I entered high school, because of scheduling conflicts, I never took advantage of the art course offered. Now, in this class, the written guidelines to drawing a profile were a real help. I drew an oval and then ran a vertical line down the right side to guide me in drawing the facial features, then proceeded according to guidelines and instruction. Being a novice, I was very pleased with the outcome of this drawing." —STUDENT BOB PINGARRON

Homework

Look for more paintings of profiles. Copying them can be fun and productive. If you didn't collect enough inspiration from your first trip to the library, go on another treasure hunt. Find family members to model while watching television. The profile face in repose is what you need, so avoid drawing during sports play-offs; too many excited expressions there!

These drawings show how varied the contour line is from person to person in portraying nose length, brow angle, and how much the mouth and chin protrude.
DRAWINGS BY STUDENTS REBECCA SMITH (LEFT) AND PATRICIA P. SPOOR (BELOW)

"I've learned that it all has to do with the shapes. It's not, 'This is my son' or anything like that. Just start to look at what's there in front of you."
—STUDENT KATHLEEN LEITAO

Expanding Value Technique: Conté

"Right now, a moment of time is fleeing by.
Capture its reality!"

—PAUL CÉZANNE

Conté crayon is a clay-based medium similar to pastel, but thinner and harder than traditional pastels. A popular, long-established brand, Conté feels like a more durable, denser charcoal. You rub the side of the square stick on paper to obtain values, and use the point or long edge to draw contour lines. Conté yields a gauzy mark, with a darker range than charcoal. It's also more permanent and less easily erased. Rely on your experience with charcoal technique to derive the most from this product.

Conté strokes are comparable to continuous subtle scrubbing movements, applied while traveling across the page.

When my students learned that I was writing this book, they lobbied for me to include Conté instruction in it. In the classroom, after some groans that greet the introduction of any new materials, beginners have found Conté very expressive and more accessible than they thought it would be.

Conté subject matter in class is drapery, a choice that is also met with a chorus of groans: "Cloth has wrinkles, and it's going to be so hard to draw!" But beginners soon find that drapery quickly disappears as the subject and *shapes* come to the forefront. Not every crinkle and wrinkle has to be depicted by any means, and fabric is so variable, that missing a few shapes here and there isn't noticeable.

As for the kind of fabric, choose only a solid-colored cloth, preferably in a medium value; avoid dark colors. In terms of size, use a piece of cloth that can be easily managed when you drape it; instructions for draping follow a little later.

But before you try your hand at drapery, start with a Conté sampler on newsprint to get a feel for this new medium.

"Once I got going, I liked Conté a bit more than charcoal because it didn't go away on you. It didn't smudge and smear."

—STUDENT ANN PORFILIO

OPPOSITE:

DRAWING BY STUDENT
JIM HOHORST

EXERCISE: CONTÉ SAMPLER

Hold Conté much as you do charcoal. Your thumb is on one side of the square stick, middle finger on the other side, index finger on the top edge, slightly to the right for righties, the reverse for lefties. Your index finger will exert downward pressure, thumb and middle finger, side-to-side movements. Adjust your grip if you feel uncomfortable. The black stick will yield intense darks, but to get them, you have to push.

1 Start by snapping off about a third of the 2-1/2" stick. Then rub one side of the small piece on paper to soften it a bit. Working on newsprint, make a variety of value marks by rubbing with the side of this smaller piece, changing the pressure as you work. Use this smaller piece for all the steps that follow.

CONTÉ SAMPLER. The Conté applications shown here are described in the accompanying exercises. Refer to these examples as you build your own sampler.

2 Remember the ribbon-candy exercise in the charcoal sampler (page 92)? Try that here.

3 Make a value scale. Start by rubbing to make a very black square, then gradually release pressure as you move gradually away from the square. Do three more of these: one with up-and-down movement; one with side-to-side application; one with a diagonal slant.

4 Draw with the tip to produce very delicate lines.

5 Use one of the lengthwise edges of the stick to draw some lines. Pull it toward you or push it away, and see the line change from thick to thin.

6 For a soft, expressive line, try this "Special Grip": Move your index finger to the center front edge of your stick; tilt it up a bit and draw with the front end only.

7 Smudge some marks (not as easily done as with charcoal). Try erasing with Pink Pearl; bear down hard and wiggle, rather than wipe at the surface layer. Conté will erase, but may leave a slightly greasy-looking edge.

8 Lean on one side of the stick to make crisp edges, then use the middle of the stick, or lessen pressure, to make a soft edge.

9 Make a rectangular shape of soft gray with the stick's flat side. Deepen the values next to one side, rubbing in a crisply defined edge. Soften the other side of the rectangle with small, diagonal movements.

10 Draw two parallel lines a few inches apart and about 4" long. Leave some paper untouched inside this column shape. Stroke in values on the inside of each line. Deepen values right next to the lines. Soften inside edges of both value applications. This exercise creates the kind of spatial change that is the basis for dimension in folds.

Building Conté Values Gradually

Imagine you're taking a walk on a foggy day. In the distance, something approaches. At first, all you see is a pale, indistinct gray shape. As it comes closer, you see contrast in the middle range and enough definition of edges to recognize a person. By the time the person is closer, high-contrast values, sharp edges, and specific details have emerged. Keep this progression in mind when you work with this medium.

EXERCISE: CONTÉ DRAWING OF DRAPED FABRIC

Create several "poses" for your fabric and make a series of drawings. If you can't pin fabric to a wall, hang it on a hook, doorknob, or over a chair arm. A drawing board is helpful for this exercise. Clip several pieces of newsprint to it as a cushion, then rest the bottom on your lap, the back against a table edge. If you don't have a drawing board, substitute your 14"-x-17" drawing pad for extra support (instead of a newsprint pad, which tends to collapse easily). Light your setup to bring out the shapes of folds. If your draping gets supercomplicated, reduce the number of folds to simplify the project. In this exercise, just try drawing contours accurately, but not perfectly. If you get lost, begin again where you can find a clear line to follow, and build in that area.

1 Begin with light marks to softly define the shapes you see. Place your drawing next to the fabric; step back to evaluate, to see if it's congruent with your model.

2 Use contour drawing to document folds, which radiate from tension points where the fabric is hung, pinned, or caught. Don't outline the whole shape first. Build in areas as you record folds.

3 Move from the top of your drawing downward, letting gravity pull your hand gradually along your paper as you "go with the flow," transcribing edges.

4 Using the flat side of your Conté, apply all shadow shapes in the same light-to-middle range. Let your stick move along the shapes you see, rubbing in values lightly. Bring the stick right up to contour lines and press in tightly to define sharp-edged shadow shapes.

5 You don't need to fill in all folds or shadows. If some folds are completed and others just suggested, as in some of the most interesting drawings, the viewer's imagination is engaged.

As these drapery drawings illustrate so well, dark values make areas seem to recede, which in turn, make lighter areas appear to move forward. The greater the contrast between dark and light, accompanied by transitional middle values, the greater the illusion of depth. STUDENT DRAWINGS BY PAM HEBERTON (TOP) AND KRISTEN NIMR (BOTTOM)

Black and White Conté on Gray Paper

Working on gray paper is unique in that it supplies the middle gray for you—comparable to the ground you created in charcoal, but here, that middle value is built into the paper. In other words, let your gray paper stand in for color application where you want to place middle values. You'll be adding white lightly in selected light areas. You'll also be extending your value range, adding more opaque white in selected light areas, deeper blacks in dark areas. Here's a **Summary of Essentials:**

- *Test your gray pastel paper, which has a different texture on each side: one smoother, one rougher. Rub your small piece of black Conté on both sides, then choose the side whose texture you prefer.*

- *Soften your **white Conté** on newsprint so you can see your white test marks easily. Add some black Conté, and let it overlap the white. You'll get an opaque gray—just what you* don't *want—because it's too close to the gray of your paper. This test alerts you to the degree of mix to avoid.*

- *Since your pastel sheet (19" × 25") needs support, either use a half-sheet on your drawing board with a newsprint cushion, or trim the sheet down to fit into your drawing pad (14" × 17"), then **tape your pastel paper** to the inside of the pad. Don't use the cardboard backing or the slick cover; both surfaces are too hard for Conté.*

- ***Arrange and light** your draped cloth.*

- ***Begin underdrawing lightly with black Conté,** rubbing in the edges you see.*

- *After stepping back to evaluate, begin an abbreviated contour drawing of the major folds, and add **shadow values** lightly, without covering too much paper.*

- *Evaluate from a distance. Where you see bright light on a fold, you will let **untouched gray paper** make the transition between highlight and shadow.*

- *Squinting, pick out three **brightest, lightest areas** on your fabric. Very lightly rub them in with your white Conté, as though they were thin veiling. Step back to see how they look from a distance. Then put in the rest of the highlight areas, keeping everything the same faint, light value.*

- ***Accent lightest and darkest** areas. Those should be most opaque, so you can't see paper texture. They are also least erasable. Pick out the three darkest areas and press harder with black to create opacity. After stepping back to evaluate your finished drawing, if needed, add more brilliance to the white with a firmer application.*

Homework

Once you're familiar with Conté, extend your subject matter to a favorite item made of unpatterned cloth. After that, don't limit your subject matter. This expressive medium suits as many subjects as your can come up with.

Other approaches to try with Conté: Go over the shapes in your drawing with a moistened towel, as though you were painting with a brush; the Conté will dissolve into a sort of wet paint. Or use your Pink Pearl vigorously; its smearing also creates a painterly look. Treat each drawing as a learning tool that may have areas you didn't get quite right—but will feel more comfortable with the next time. Have fun with what you think is unsalvageable art. Push hard into the paper to create a more forceful, dynamic application of values right over that first drawing. You'll see that you can reinvent a drawing with the intense black values Conté can provide.

"When you're up close, it can look funny, like it's not anything, but standing back, you see the parts come together— from one shape to another."

—STUDENT AMY MILLER

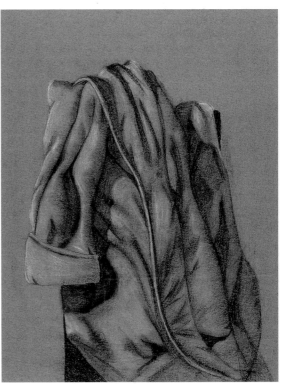

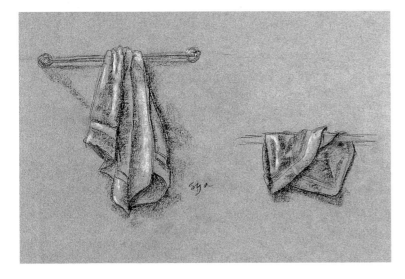

A precious daughter's favorite dress, your favorite coat, or even a washcloth observed during a bubble bath (this student completed that drawing a day later, sitting in her empty tub!) can provide inspiration as they did for these three artists. —STUDENT DRAWINGS BY ANGELA LOWY (TOP LEFT), NANCY OPGAARD (TOP RIGHT), AND SHERRY ARTEMENKO (LEFT)

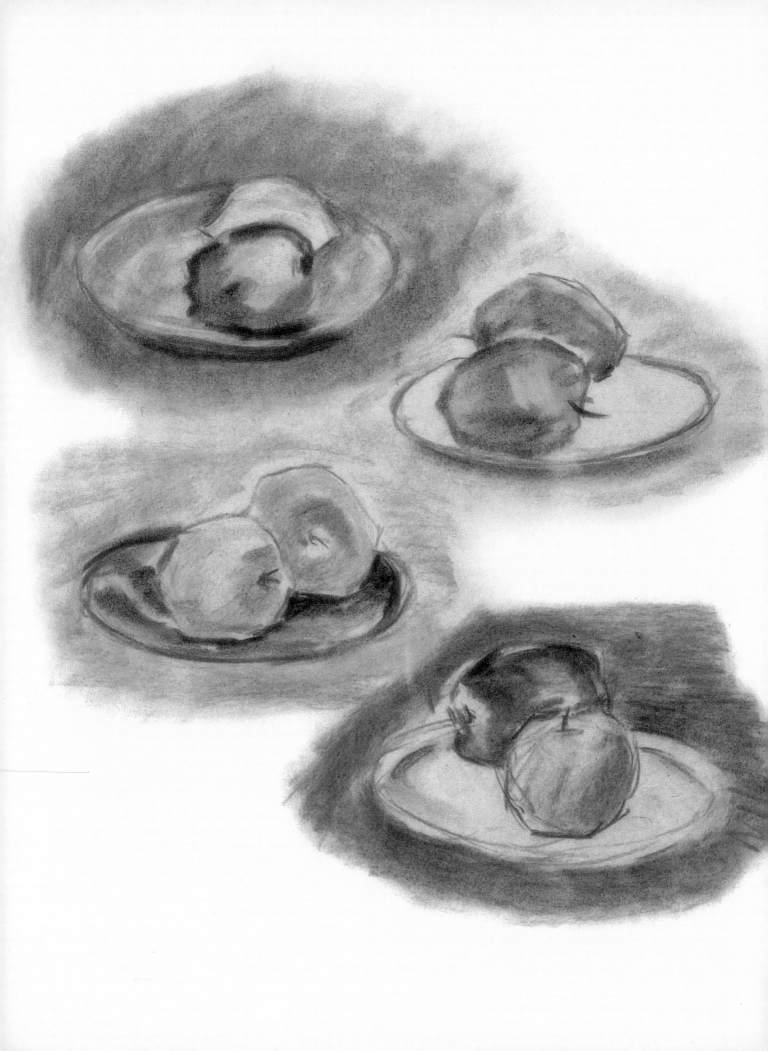

Still Life

"Every man's work—in literature, music, or pictures—is always a portrait of himself, and the more he tries to conceal himself, the more clearly will his character appear . . . "

—SAMUEL BUTLER

Before concentrating on creating still life, let's review just what it is. Still lifes are composed of related objects that can't get up and walk off. "Related" refers to an aesthetic relationship created by the artist among items that harmonize visually, but not necessarily with a constant theme such as "My Twine Collection" or "Squashes I Have Known." Rather, as long as the items are inanimate, you can make disparate choices, in as simple or complex, stately or bizarre a still life as your personal taste dictates. If you are drawing several objects, your challenge will be to make them hold together as part of an aesthetic group.

Once again, hunt for "beloved" subject matter that has a strong appeal for you—but in the case of a still life, choose objects that are pleasing to you as a group.

Still life is really composed of several individual drawings. The challenge becomes how to make that assembly of drawings hold together effectively, as part of an inseparable group.

Your still life can be as polished or informal as you like. Some beginners love taking a long time to create very detailed, meticulously rendered objects. Others feel comfortable with a direct, spontaneous approach that is not so time-consuming. Neither is better, wrong, nor preferable. Yet, we all have a tendency to eye the working style of someone else and say with a sigh, either, "I wish I had the patience to . . . " or "I wish I were more free . . . " The best approach is simply to take your still-life projects to whatever level of finish works best for you.

Here's your chance to tap into all the basics you've practiced in the preceding chapters, while reinforcing and adding to them with some expanded techniques.

SUPPLIES FOR THIS CHAPTER
2B, 2H, 6B, 6H pencils
vine charcoal
newsprint pad
14"-×-17" drawing pad
6"-×-8" drawing pad
Pink Pearl eraser
clip-on light
drawing board

"I saw how tentative I was in my work, and I was so locked into making it 'perfect.'"

—STUDENT ANITA ST. MARIE

OPPOSITE: DRAWINGS BY STUDENT GENIE BOURNE

Added Tools for Still Life

Lightest to darkest values are stacked from top row to bottom, using pencils 6H, 2H, 2B, 6B. Each scribble moves horizontally as the value scale of each pencil goes from dark to light.

BELOW: Cast shadows as strong as these can be as important a component of a still-life composition as the objects themselves. DRAWING BY STUDENT ANNE OSSO PORCO

If you're working in pencil, broaden your range of values. Along with the 2B and 2H pencils you've used earlier, add the softer 6B and harder 6H, which will enable you to incorporate a more dramatic range of grays. There are places where these expanded options will be an asset. Dark shadows on an eggplant call for 6B; shadows on an egg, 6H. While 2B pencils are fine for shadow values on dark skin tones, a 6B may be best for very dark surfaces. Although obsessed pencil lovers would urge using many more pencils, in my opinion, only the four I've named are needed for the still lifes you'll create.

EXPANDING VALUE

As shown in my example, make a controlled scribble with each of your four pencils. Exert pressure as you begin each one, then release gradually to create a value scale. Stack the scribbles on top of one another, from lightest to darkest: 6H, 2H, 2B, 6B. You should see a value scale emerge from top to bottom, light to dark, as well as the value scale of each pencil horizontally, from dark to light. Just as you did earlier with your 2H and 2B pencils, use your 6H to smooth out the 6B texture. Since darker marks are harder to erase, it makes sense to hold back the darkest intensity of the 6B until the final stages. Make a scribble to approximate the value of each object you've chosen for your still life.

UNDERDRAWING

No matter which medium you use, when composing a still life, underdrawing is useful. As you learned in Chapter 3, a light sketch provides a foundation, ensuring that effort isn't wasted putting pencil layers on items that are crooked or unintentionally tilting. But your underdrawing must be checked out by viewing it up on a wall to be sure nothing's askew before you develop the work further. Unfortunately, beginners are often in what I call "Art Denial"—and when homework goes up on the wall, they suddenly see for the first time that the wonderfully rendered still lifes they spent so much time on are listing like lunch on the *Titanic!* With careful preparation, you can avoid that fate.

POSITIONING OBJECTS IN SPACE

Think of still-life objects as actors on a stage, each in position relative to the others and to you, the audience/viewer. Some are closer to you, some farther back. Determine those positions in space by using a level. Hold it over your still-life setup and lower it slowly, noting the position of objects according to height. Pick up additional reference information on the way down. Repeat the process from beneath to determine the front-to-back progression in space. The first to touch the level is closest; the second is next-closest, and so on, to the back. Don't make the mistake of drawing all your objects as if they were actors taking their curtain call—lined up straight across the stage.

If your still life is on a tabletop, apply what you learned about angles in Chapter 3 in order to draw them accurately. Tables are usually drawn from a slightly overhead vantage point so you can see what's on them. You'll see them either in one-point or two-point perspective, depending on where you're sitting. One-point means you're directly in front of the table; two-point means one leg and the corresponding corner of the table are the closest parts to you.

Although understanding perspective thoroughly is critical to an artist's development, I believe it's a subject better left for intermediate-level studies. The concept of a vanishing point—where parallel lines converge at eye level, or on the horizon line—is important in drawing landscapes and cityscapes, particularly, but since that subject matter is beyond the scope of this book, the terms are just mentioned in passing and in material indicating what to do and what *not* to do in handling tabletop perspective.

SKETCH FREEHAND FIRST

I suggest that you sketch your tabletop freehand first. Perhaps you will be able to draw angles accurately from observation only, and then, to check yourself, simply apply level and plumbline at every corner you observe that isn't at a right angle to help you see it better and replicate what you see. If you aren't satisfied with your freehand results, use the steps outlined ahead to increase your undertanding. Employ the strategies for drawing angles and sighting that were covered in the countertop exercise in Chapter 3.

CHECKLIST FOR TABLETOP DRAWINGS

- *Place a table in two-point position relative to you (one table leg and corner are the closest parts to you).*

- *Use your level, holding your pencil horizontally just under the front corner of the table. Squint to see wedges of negative space between the level and the front angles along the table edge, right and left.*
- *Sketch a horizontal line corresponding to your level on paper.*
- *Sketch in your angles at the front corner. Remeasure to make sure they aren't drawn too open.*

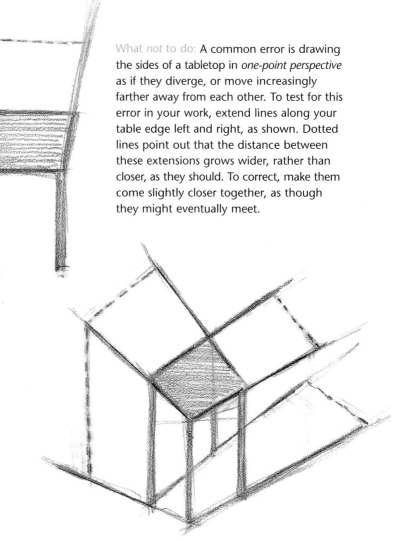

What *not* to do: A common error is drawing the sides of a tabletop in *one-point perspective* as if they diverge, or move increasingly farther away from each other. To test for this error in your work, extend lines along your table edge left and right, as shown. Dotted lines point out that the distance between these extensions grows wider, rather than closer, as they should. To correct, make them come slightly closer together, as though they might eventually meet.

What *not* to do: A common error in drawing *two-point perspective* is making the back edges of a table seem to lift up, as if about to fly, with edges growing farther apart from their parallel partners. To test for this error, extend the parallel lines on four sides of the tabletop (the illustration also shows what happens to the rest of the table). Dotted lines shown point out the unwanted divergence of these lines, when they should be parallel or growing closer to each other, as though they might eventually meet.

- *Determine your scale by sketching in the entire length of the shortest side of the table; the size is your choice and determines the scale of the whole table.*
- *Define the end of the short edge by sketching a vertical line at the end of the short edge where the leg is.*
- *Sight on the horizontal from front corner to end of leg on the shortest side, to find a measurement for the shortest side. You'll be sighting along the bottom line of a triangle.*
- *Estimate the longer side relative to the shorter one and draw that in.*
- *Use your level to verify angles of right and left corners. Extend those angles until they meet, forming the back corner. And now—you have a tabletop!*
- *Apply sighting techniques to determine the length and angle of the front leg*

and relative position of back legs, if you wish to include those. The front leg will appear longest.
- *Use the same approach and tools for a one-point drawing. Only two angles at front right and left corners require measurement, and they will be of equal size.*

CONSTRUCTIVE EVALUATION

Put your table sketch on the wall. Sit in the position from which you drew it to make your evaluation. Does the tabletop look flipped up? If so, the angles are too open. If the top is too flat, the angles are probably too closed. In either case, review front angles and correct them. You are in the process of discovering how this works, and as is often the case, you'll need to adjust your sketch.

DRAWING BY STUDENT
ANN PORFILIO

Arrange your final still life. Light it to bring out dimension and interesting patterns. Although the steps ahead pertain to any medium, using pencil may make the following easier to absorb the first time. After that, pen, wash, charcoal, or Conté, alone or in combination, await!

"I was hesitant to show what I had done. My drawing was in very light strokes. But as the weeks passed, I noticed a tendency to use bolder strokes."

—STEPHEN MONAHAN

STEP 1: UNDERDRAWING. Lightly sketch your still-life objects. I used a 2H pencil to search out shapes, focusing on their relationships to each other, along both horizontal and vertical sight lines. "Drawing through" (page 43) is helpful here. Check for scale and symmetry, so you won't build on a faulty foundation. This may be messy, so clean up with an eraser, once you settle on shapes, to prepare for the next step.

STEP 2: DEVELOPING FEATURES. Develop contour lines, adding specifics. Lightly indicate highlights. Squint to see basic value relationships. Scribble in local values, then add shadows on objects and reflected light, if any. Leave paper untouched for lightest areas and highlights, filling in around them. Break up or subdue any rigid, too-dark outlines if you want a still life that looks dimensional. I added 2B here to all areas but the empty portions of the wine glass, where I filled in with 2H. Surfaces and transitions are still rough at this point.

CONSTRUCTIVE EVALUATION

Before taking the final step, sit with your still-life setup between you and your artwork so you can see both from your drawing position. Address any areas that need strengthening or correction. Determine:

- *Are your values generally accurate?*
- *Can you improve your drawing with some darker values?*
- *Can you simply apply pressure to your 2B, or do you need a 6B?*
- *Does your drawing lack the excitement and verve you had hoped it would have?*

Problems with value application and dimension are covered in Chapter 4; solutions to questions about charcoal are in Chapter 6; Conté, in Chapter 9.

"I worry that my painstaking, meticulous approach sacrifices spontaneity and flair. I admire some of my classmates' works which would not have received high grades for accuracy, but which have a real pizzazz."

—STUDENT GEORGE E. STEVENS

STRATEGIES FOR ADDING DARKER VALUES

In a still life, when adding darker values, you need to consider the group as a whole. Especially with the bold capacity of the 6B in your toolbag, if you darken one area with it, avoid isolating that spot, or it will become the focus of your drawing, riveting the viewer's eye where it shouldn't be. For balance, add darkest tones to a few other areas—in edges or shadows, to pull attention into other parts of your drawing. If you're not sure where, pick three areas that would benefit from darker values. If you're nervous about it, work in small steps—or, save this strategy for another still life.

"This was my first art course. When we got to still life, my big problem was deciding what to do. I made six different setups and tried them out first in charcoal. My final setup related to the type of food I cook regularly, and was pleasing to me. Over time, I studied, erased, and redrew. My tool of choice, the pencil, is a gracious medium, accommodating precision while tolerating changes. At this point, it suits me perfectly. I was surprised and pleased with the result"

—STUDENT ANN PORTFILIO

KNOWING WHEN TO STOP

"When am I finished?" When you ask yourself that question, it's a gut reaction that's worth listening to—and probably means you're nearly there. Many beginners spend days working on one piece, enjoying the process of getting lost in time, focused on the development of a single drawing. It's not hard to become obsessive—but beware of overworking a drawing. Instead, direct that energy to something new. Tack your present picture up in a protected area, where you can revisit it from time to time to decide if and when it's finished.

Before going to the final step in your still life, another option to consider is leaving part of it deliberately unfinished. That approach allows viewers to be in on the process of completing your picture with their own imaginations.

"I have come to realize that if I try to draw an exact rendition, I set myself up for failure and frustration. What I try to do now is draw my best interpretation of what I see."

—STUDENT RITA WALKER COPPING

144

STEP 3: FINALIZING. Refine surfaces and value transitions with finer, multidirectional pencil scribbling, adding details and value contrasts as needed. I added 6B here, concentrating on the dark wine bottle, and added 6B accents elsewhere, working on top of foundation values with fine scribbling to reflect the objects' surfaces. Smudging with finger and eraser helps smooth surfaces and blend value transitions. Note the value shapes added in negative spaces as a guide to applying them in your own work (see "Filling the Void," page 147).

Further Refinement of Your Still Life

Yes, there are still some things to ask yourself before declaring your still life absolutely finished:

- *Does your eye drift to the surrounding blank negative space where nothing is going on?*
- *Do the objects look isolated from each other, rather than related?*
- *Do you find your eye pulled to the horizon line, or sides of the picture, rather than where you want it?*
- *Is the mood of the work remote, or cold—not the feeling you intended?*

This pitcher and casserole (top) seem to float in space. When grounded (bottom) by cast shadows and the suggestion of a tabletop, the two objects are transformed from separate drawings into a cohesive still life.
DRAWINGS BY STUDENT JANE WOLANSKY

If you answered *yes* to any of above, be assured there are remedies ahead.

The drawing you've just made was a learning exercise, not the culmination of all there is to know about still life. Keep in mind that you're in the midst of a creative process that unfolds over time. This process involves learning what appeals to you and what doesn't. It means giving yourself the room to try what you don't think you'll like, just in case there are surprises in store for you there.

With the still life you've just completed, maybe your drawing came out really well. Great, if that's so. Just keep in mind that the longest time invested doesn't necessarily guarantee greatest success. Sometimes a quick sketch works better than the drawing you slaved over. Sometimes a meticulous piece is satisfying, other times the labor leaves you just plain irritated. In either case, success or failure in a still-life drawing has a lot to do with its composition. Let's go there now.

COMPOSITION

Composition can remedy the problems you may have identified in your final evaluation. It is the tool that can bring the elements of your still life together more effectively. Beginners are usually focused on drawing objects, and less concerned with the role played by the space around objects. The tension between positive space (real objects) and negative space (shapes around the objects) is the basis for composition. The attention you've given to the positive shapes can make the negative spaces seem especially blank in contrast. Large negative spaces often pull attention away from the drawn objects.

Good composition gives a drawing its overall appeal. There is no single right way to compose a picture, but there is always the most effective one, once you decide what's interesting to you. You create your composition to focus the viewer's eye on what matters most to you. For example, if three people are shown a bouquet to draw, one might focus on a single flower, another a bug on a leaf, and the third might draw the entire bouquet.

Where to put your focus? When composing a still life, put your focal point in the area where viewers automatically look to find the most significant subject matter: in the center–but not the absolute center–of your drawing. Then, there are some simple tricks to help you deal effectively with the role of the space around your focal point.

FILLING THE VOID

To prevent negative space from being boring, break up an empty expanse by adding subtle value shapes (nicknamed *schmutz* in my class), a technique that has been used widely in drawing and painting for centuries. Preview this technique on your own work by looking at your still life and imagining that the objects there emit a light-gray magnetic field in the negative space, like breath on a cold day. The shape of the field would be like an asymmetrical halo around the objects, echoing their contours, with a slightly lighter value border between it and surrounding shapes. Suddenly, there's something interesting going on there as this energetic shape vitalizes boring negative space. It can act as bridge to connect still-life objects, as well. A subtle, light application of values is all that's needed to make that shape appear.

Above, the shadow shape cast from apple to bottle bridges the gap between them and creates a compositional link. At left, a faint value shape is more effective than a single horizontal line to indicate a table edge, as seen here. STUDENT DRAWINGS, FROM TOP, BY MARY JO FUSARO AND JIM HOHORST

147

Making Connections, Creating Harmony

One of my students said her still life looked as though each object belonged in separate drawings. How could she get them to look related? She'd drawn only the objects, and hadn't dealt with the tabletop and surrounding space. When she applied subtle values in those areas, her recognizable, individual style, or touch—also known as an artist's "hand"—energized her still life by knitting positive and negative spaces together.

While the artist's personal, sensitive hand can unify a drawing, conversely, lines drawn in an unfelt, "I'm bored" manner, can have a negative impact on a drawing, resulting in disharmony. This doesn't mean that some lines can't be quick and more casual, even within a polished still life. But caring and involvement, translated directly through the hand, seem to be decisive in making all the elements of a still life connect harmoniously.

Another consideration in creating harmony in a still life is the proximity of objects to one another. The space between them becomes activated if they are somewhat close, or in intimate contact. Still-life elements can also be connected by values taken from the surface and/or background as a unifying bridge. Cast shadows or light also provide links.

Harmony means elements of your picture are in balance as integrated parts of an entity, but not necessarily quiet, serene, or soft. You can create a harmonious arrangement of the most ragged, active elements. When balanced, the viewer's eye keeps moving over the composition, rather than being led out of town or stuck in a large negative space. Think of a successful composition as akin to a well-played game of pinball. The object is to return to big payoff areas toward the center, and move freely around the drawing without getting stuck.

EXIT LINES

We have established that the focal point of a composition should be near the center. Therefore, most effective still lifes keep high-contrast areas and emphatic lines in that area. What about the sides of the drawing? Strong exit lines can be like a posse leading out of town, which is impossible not to follow with the eye. Instead, to keep your viewers returning to your chosen focus, soften contour lines and value contrasts on the outskirts of the significant elements of your drawing. As the artist, that decision is yours; it doesn't matter if the object doesn't actually disappear.

Strong horizontal lines—in a still life, usually in the form of a tabletop—not only draw the eye out of the picture but rivet it as though to the horizon, especially if the line is very bold. To maintain central focus, keep that tabletop line soft, diminishing it where it wanders far from the subject.

THUMBNAIL SKETCHES ESTABLISH BOUNDARIES

Beginners intuitively give boundaries to their still life once "schmutz"—those useful value shapes—are added to negative space. An overall border, or frame, emerges in a subtle way, determined by the outside edges of those shapes. However, even such subtle boundaries require planning, which can be made easier by using a primary compositional tool: the thumbnail sketch—a preview device that helps you avoid stepping into common compositional problems. These shorthand sketches are simple, blunt, and undeveloped. They're called thumbnails because they're usually small.

Drawing a frame around your thumbnail establishes decisive borders to define negative-space shapes clearly. In effect, you determine the borders of your still life rather than accept the edges of the paper as the boundary authority. Artists often do several charcoal thumbnails to see which boundaries work best for a drawing and arrangement of negative space. As a general rule, reducing excess negative space strengthens a composition, bringing attention to the drawing's focal point. Charcoal is preferred for thumbnails because it is so direct, decisive, and easy to alter. Those qualities may be unappealing to you if you like to work slowly and want everything to be polished and in place. The mere look of messiness may signal ineptness to you, but the ability to size up all elements quickly to capture the essence of what you see is a skill worth developing. So take advantage of the following exercise to explore the benefits of working with thumbnail sketches.

"Charcoal let me get down on paper quickly what I thought I was seeing."
—STUDENT ANN PORFILIO

A charcoal thumbnail sketch like this is an excellent way to plan a still-life composition and define its borders. Thumbnail "frames" are notations for the artist, but do not appear explicitly in a larger drawing based on them. DRAWING BY STUDENT SHERRY ARTEMENKO

EXERCISE: THUMBNAIL SKETCH
A thumbnail should include basic shapes and important values. If a black olive is the darkest thing in your still life of cauliflowers and eggs, even though it's small, account for it in your thumbnail. A common pitfall is making a teeny detailed drawing rather than a fast, direct impression that gets to the point. Work quickly. It will force you to let go of conscious control and perfectionism. Use charcoal and newsprint, and have a timer with a loud bell on hand to keep you moving—no more than fifteen minutes for each thumbnail sketch. Refer to the accompanying student examples as you review your own.

"I forced myself to work fast, even though it was really hard, because I was into doing detail. Everyone wound up liking those fast ones best."

—STUDENT HELEN LOBRANO

1 Set up a casual still life, one you don't have a lot invested in. Use newsprint with your drawing board or your 14"-x-17" pad.
2 Set your timer for fifteen minutes. Draw your first thumbnail on about half of a sheet. Include the whole still life.
3 After the timer goes off, draw a frame around your work. Take your time with this part. Step back to see if you need to adjust the frame to trim unnecessary negative space.
4 Set your timer for ten minutes. Draw your second thumbnail on about a quarter of a sheet (as below). Focus on just an interesting aspect of the still life, not the whole setup. Add frame marks and evaluate.
5 Set your timer for ten minutes or less. Choose an unusual view of the still life—perhaps cropped at an odd place, and draw your frame there. Evaluate.

"I actually really like these drawings, because when I look at all of my work together, they have more energy. The others were more static." —STUDENT KIM NIGHTINGALE

Adjusting the border on her thumbnail sketch reinforces the focal point of this artist's still life. DRAWING BY STUDENT STEPHANIE SEIDEL

This artist has cropped out one section of the larger thumbnail (above) to see how she likes it as a closeup (right). Which do you prefer? DRAWINGS BY STUDENT SHERRY ARTEMENKO

You may find potential compositions within a larger sketch, as this artist has done (below). DRAWING BY STUDENT JANE WOLANSKY

"I was more successful in timed exercises where I had to react and not think too much. I find if I am reworking something too much, I need to set it aside and start over." —STUDENT JIM HOHORST

This artist used pencil in her small sketchbook to try out a composition before rendering it in bold charcoal values. DRAWINGS BY STUDENT RITA WALKER COPPING

USING A VIEWFINDER

Similar to a thumbnail sketch, a camera's viewfinder also creates compositions, letting you cut out of the frame what you don't want. Look through your camera and "take pictures" without film to reinforce your sense of framing a still-life image. Take closeups to experiment with their impact. An empty slide mount is also a wonderful viewfinder. Two L-shaped cutouts allow you to make an expanding and contracting frame held in two hands—or compose your still life with the viewfinder that's always right at hand: your own fingers held up to form a frame.

CONSTRUCTIVE EVALUATION

Step back to review your sketches. If you have large areas of negative space, crop them or add some "schmutz" to break them up. Or do you need to add more space around objects? Rearrange your still life and try the exercise again. If you dislike the "mess" of thumbnails, give yourself time to get used to the results. Keep them. You may find appealing small drawings within larger sketches.

Look for nice arrangements of positive and negative space in the drawings you've done so far. As you look, think of your paper's edges as electrified fences: harmless until you get near them—then, watch out! Compositional tools are critical, and by now, you know why: to keep attention on the focal point of your still life. But there are other reasons why they are important; you must dictate where the creative space of your picture begins and ends. If you don't, a framer will, and can ruin the look of your work. As you develop as an artist, composition will play an increasingly significant role. Even now, an awareness of composition will add to the quality of your informal drawings, as well as deepen your understanding of the art you see in museums and galleries.

One sketch (above) led to a finished drawing (right) when this artist discovered the subject she really wanted to draw within a sketch. DRAWINGS BY STUDENT BARBARA KOPS

153

Problem Solvers

Here are some common problems in composing drawings, and helpful solutions to them. See if any of these problems pertain to the drawings you've created so far, and refer to the solutions in the future to reinforce your understanding of composition fundamentals.

RIGHT: **PROBLEM.** Large spaces around an object make it look lonely and isolated.

FAR RIGHT: **SOLUTION.** Reduce the negative space if that's not your intent.

RIGHT: **PROBLEM.** Tight negative space seems to pressure the subject or make it look squeezed.

FAR RIGHT: **SOLUTION.** Increase negative space or let the subject exit cleanly. Avoid ending just at the edge or cropping out only a tiny bit.

RIGHT: **PROBLEM.** Equal spaces look boring and predictable. The eye is a hedonist and wants to be entertained!

FAR RIGHT: **SOLUTION.** Place your subject matter off center. Use value "schmutz" in negative spaces to make them look different from each other.

154

Homework

Use your small pad this week with composition in mind. Remember you can alter the basic pad format to any size just by drawing new borders. If you like the process of developing a polished still life, thumbnails can help you work through possibilities in a visual shorthand. Maybe you'll find an arrangement you'd like to take into a more developed drawing.

"My son is seven and just started playing the saxophone, so I had a special feeling about it. I like the way the mood is conveyed in the negative space, because it adds so much to the drawing—almost like a halo around things—more atmosphere, more presence."
—STUDENT JANE WOLANSKY

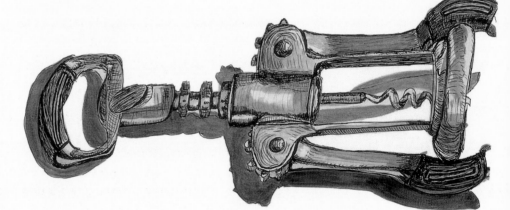

> "When you're raising children, you never actually get to finish anything. To actually do something and complete it and get a result is mindblowing! It's the first time in twelve years I've gotten to do something like that."
> —STUDENT HELEN LOBRANO

> "Even though I may have problems with aspects of all of the pieces, it's still fulfilling to have something there that I could never have done before. It gives me hope that I may be able to learn more and get better."
> —STUDENT KIM NIGHTINGALE

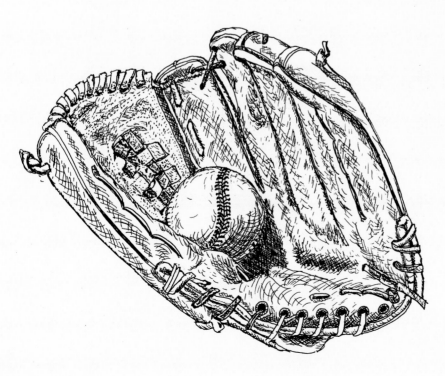

> "I'm pleased to have laid to rest the evil ghost of my fourth-grade art teacher, who looked at my earnest attempt to draw a person and announced for the entire class to hear, 'That's a stupid, asinine drawing!' (Some things you never forget.)"
> —STUDENT AL ROBERTS

Your Inner Aesthetic

*"I celebrate myself, and sing myself,
And what I assume you shall assume,
For every atom belonging to me as good belongs to you."*
—WALT WHITMAN

In my classroom, we do our last exercise as homework before our last class, and discuss the reactions and discoveries while celebrating with food and drink. After you've followed the same procedure, why not fix yourself a snack and *celebrate yourself!*

EXERCISE: FINDING YOURSELF IN YOUR ART
An aesthetic profile can appear when you have a body of work to review, which is the basis of our final exercise. That doesn't mean that what you see reflects who you are as an artist forever, but it will give you a sense of who you are as an artist now. The picture literally emerges and develops with your skills—if you simply keep going.

1　Place all your work on the floor in a line, if that's possible, from the beginning wire drawings to the final pieces you did. Look over the progression to see how your work developed.
2　Now reduce the collection to seven favorites, and remove the rest. Move those seven into another arrangement on the floor or on a wall, if possible—not in a straight line.
3　Find your favorite piece. Why do you like it best?
4　What is your favorite medium?
5　What were your discoveries? When were those moments that a light bulb went on in your head, either about yourself, a technique, or a medium? Does your arrangement itself tell a story? For example, is your favorite drawing in the middle? Drawings to the left or right of your favorite may indicate where you have been and where you wish to go, respectively.
6　Now turn those pieces upside down. Do you see any consistency of value range? Do you see high contrast or close, silvery, low-contrast values? Is your work especially large or small in scale? Do you see any repetition of shapes? Are your drawings still and composed or energetic and bold? Is there any noticeable rhythm to your work?

"When I reviewed all my projects, I was surprised to identify a common mood: quiet, contemplative, subdued."
—STUDENT GEORGE E. STEVENS

OPPOSITE: STUDENT DRAWINGS, FROM TOP, BY HELEN LOBRANO, KIM NIGHTINGALE, AL ROBERTS

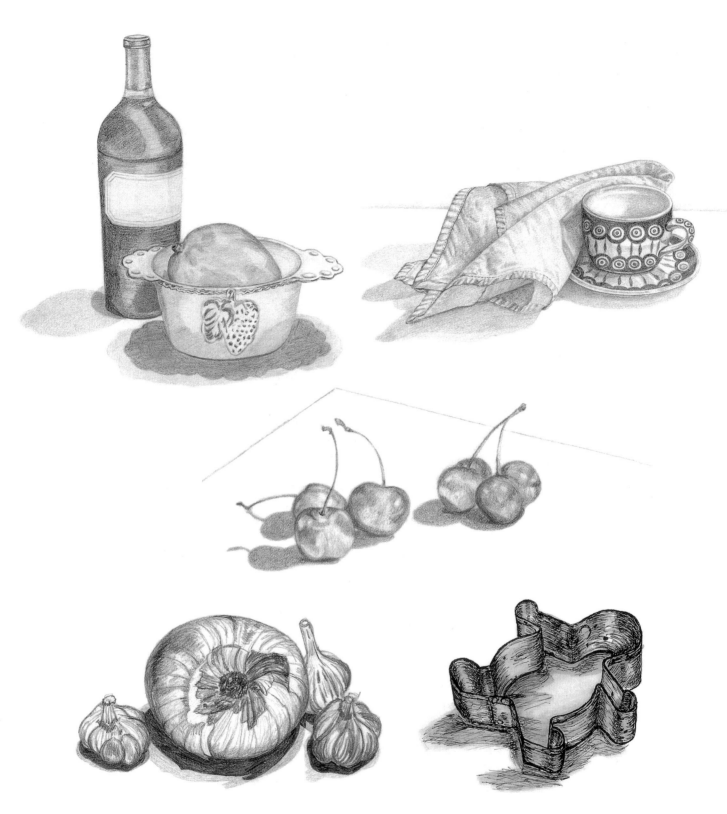

DRAWINGS BY STUDENT ANITA ST. MARIE

For the same reason that we began with upside-down drawing in Chapter 1, this upside-down viewing helps you to bypass literal identities and focus more on those underlying aesthetic components of line, shape, and value revealed by your personal interpretation. "We don't see things as they are, we see them as we are," said writer Anaïs Nin. It's that unique inner aesthetic to look for in your art. In doing so, it can be instructive to write down your findings and goals. For instance, what medium would you like to continue exploring? Do you prefer drawing faces or still lifes?

Studying the work of other artists to find the kinds of consistencies you've looked for in your own work is also a useful exercise. On the opposite page, you'll find a group of drawings by a student who is a not-quite beginner, whose work provides a vivid example of the mysterious consistencies of inner style that emerge over time, as you will find in your own work.

"A long time ago, I began to develop my art, and then abandoned it. When I began to draw again, I decided to be bold and committed and throw caution to the wind. I imagined my work would be impressionistic. I tried to draw more quickly and less detailed, but couldn't change what was coming out on paper. I was fascinated by detail. Then I uncovered my old portfolio that I had made fifteen years ago and was surprised to see the same attention to detail as today. I realized that there are certain things in us that come out, no matter what, because it's part of our innate style, our personality, or how we see things in the world.

—STUDENT ANITA ST. MARIE

AESTHETIC EVALUATION

Examine the five drawings on the opposite page to see if you can locate those aesthetic aspects that echo throughout this representative grouping of a student's work. Then compare your findings with the answers given in the box below. Consistent with our upside-down mode, they are printed that way to give you a chance to find your own answers before consulting these.

- A scallop-shaped contour is repeated in shadow shapes, the lacy edges of the pottery, the contours of cherry groupings and garlic cloves, even in the cookie cutter, which at first seems different.
- A rounded bull's-eye motif, an echo of the cherry shapes, can be seen in the middle of the onion, the mango in the bowl, and within the strawberry decoration.
- Note the similarity in the cast-shadow shapes of the napkin and the cookie cutter.
- Observe the even, silvery gray value range, with about the same amount of contrast overall—with one exception: the pen technique, which creates high contrast.

ONGOING EXPLORATIONS IN ART

This book opened with "Starting Out," so it seemed appropriate to end with "Finishing Up"—but I certainly hope that your finish here will mark the *beginning* of your ongoing explorations in art. When you set a clear goal, just as you did at the start of this book ("I want to learn to draw"), it may be easier to attain further artistic goals. Taking a class, now that you have some skills that allow you to enter at a more confident level, will help you to maintain your connection to your art. You need to protect what's emerged with a schedule that will help you to do so. Whatever your path may be, all the beginners who helped with this book join me in wishing you—Good luck!

Index